SECOND BOOK OF
MATHEMATICAL BAFFLERS

Edited by ANGELA FOX DUNN

Illustrations by ED KYSAR

DOVER PUBLICATIONS, INC.
NEW YORK

Published in Canada by General Publishing Company, Ltd., 30 Lesmill Road, Don Mills, Toronto, Ontario.
Published in the United Kingdom by Constable and Company, Ltd., 10 Orange Street, London WC2H 7EG.

This Dover edition, first published in 1983, is a new selection from the puzzles originally published between 1959 and 1971 in the magazines *Aviation Week* and *Electronic News* and collected into pamphlets titled *Problematical Recreations*, published between 1965 and 1970 by Litton Industries, Beverly Hills, California. A few corrections have been made in the present edition, for which a new introduction has also been prepared.

Book design by Barbara Effron

Manufactured in the United States of America
Dover Publications, Inc., 180 Varick Street,
New York, N.Y. 10014

Library of Congress Cataloging in Publication Data
Main entry under title:

Second book of mathematical bafflers.

Puzzles which originally appeared in Aviation week and Electronic news between 1959 and 1971 and later were collected in pamphlets titled Problematical recreations published by Litton Industries between 1965 and 1970.
    1. Mathematical recreations.   I. Dunn, Angela.
QA95.S395   1983   793.7′4   82-9473
ISBN 0-486-24352-4 (pbk.)   AACR2

INTRODUCTION

Every week in the years 1959 to 1971 an unusual small advertisement called "Problematical Recreations," featuring a mathematical puzzle, appeared in the magazines *Aviation Week* and *Electronic News;* the solution was given the following week. The series carried the logo of Litton Industries of Beverly Hills, California, the company that had initiated and continued to sponsor the campaign. Over the years "Problematical Recreations" became the most successful corporate advertising series ever presented in technical publications, winning the highest readership scores more than twenty-five times, until the publications thought it only fair to the other advertisers to withdraw the Litton ads from the judging.

It was the readers themselves who were responsible for the overwhelming success of "Problematical Recreations." Working mathematicians, engineers, scientists, and puzzle buffs from all over the United States and throughout the world continually contributed ingenious originals, new and fresh brainteasers designed to surprise and delight. It was their imaginative offerings that attracted attention and kept the puzzle series on top for a dozen years.

This second collection of the best from "Problematical Recreations" is published here for the first time, 158 new challenges for those who never saw the Litton series. Readers familiar with the collection *Mathematical Bafflers* (Dover 23961-6) will find the same organization by chapter, though the sample correspondence near the beginning of each chapter is missing here. The letters have long since been lost. Fortunately the puzzles were collected yearly in little booklets to be distributed at technical trade shows. This previously unpublished collection, representing the series' later years, is based on those booklets, which were happily preserved.

The present collection, like the first, offers a range of problems from the simple to the complex, all presented by type. There are many problems requiring no mathematical background whatsoever, and there are stumpers that will test the best mathematical minds. Try this problem (no. 135) from the chapter "Now You See It":

What property is common to the sports of rowing and tug-of-war, the planet Uranus, and a clock whose hands move at the correct rate but which gives the right time only 4 times daily?

All you need to solve it is a little reasoning. Yet the nineteen puzzles in the chapter "Permutations, Partitions, and Primes" can only be attacked by those acquainted with number theory. You will find, however, that most solutions can be reached much more readily by cleverness than by hard labor.

I was the director of "Problematical Recreations" from 1962 until its last offering in 1971, a position I could not have filled without the help of some of the best, most creative mathematicians, chiefly the late David L. Silverman of the University of California at Los Angeles, to whom I again pay tribute. David had a rare inventive bent. Many of the most ingenious puzzles in this collection, as well as in the first Dover volume of bafflers, are the product of David Silverman's highly original, superbly concise mind.

I am also indebted to dozens of followers of "Problematical Recreations" who consistently submitted intriguing posers to the series year after year, particularly the regulars: Mr. Walter Penney of Greenbelt, Maryland; Mr. Leonard A. Baljay of Cherry Hill, New Jersey; Mr. Charles Baker of Los Angeles, California; Mr. J. N. A. Hawkins of Pacific Palisades, California; Mr. William Shooman of Orange, California; Mr. Noel A. Longmore of Kent, England; and Mr. B. van Blaricum of Melbourne, Australia. Both David Silverman and Dr. Harry Lass of the California Institute of Technology helped check and evaluate each original contribution. Their assistance and advice are gratefully acknowledged.

Over the twelve years the series ran, a few problems were reprinted with permission from the publications of the Mathematical Association of America, *American Mathematical Monthly* and *Mathematics Magazine*. The editor thankfully acknowledges these contributions.

A very special thanks is due Dr. Robert Guralnick, professor of mathematics at the University of Southern California, whose assistance in compiling this second collection was invaluable.

The reader will note that several problems in this book mention the mythical country of Puevigi. The name was derived by joining three words together backwards. Once you've deciphered the message, it is hoped you will not heed it, but will instead enjoy pursuing the answers.

ANGELA FOX DUNN

CONTENTS

SAY IT WITH LETTERS
Algebraic Amusements

A Stationery Problem 1

A pencil, eraser, and notebook together cost $1.00. A notebook costs more than two pencils, and three pencils cost more than four erasers. If three erasers cost more than a notebook, how much does each cost?

2 The Goldbricker

Luke and Pete are two privates on K.P. peeling potatoes at the rate of one per minute each. They start with
the same number, but Goldbrick Luke surreptitiously
throws one potato on Pete's pile after every second one
he peels. At a certain moment Pete has twice as many
potatoes still to be peeled as Luke. Five minutes later
this ratio has increased to 7:3. When will it be three to
one?

4 • SAY IT WITH LETTERS

Position Impossible 3 ?

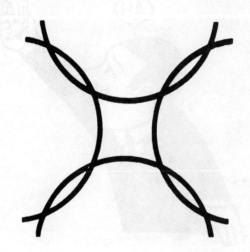

Depicted above are two interlocked hyperbolas. Impossible? You're right, but can you prove it?

4 The "Aha!" Phenomenon

If THAT = (AH) (HA), what is THAT?

Among those numbers whose literal representations in capitals consist of straight line segments only (e.g. FIVE), only one is "orthonymic," i.e., is equal to the number of segments which comprise it. Find the number.

√6 • An Uncertainty

Why not? Because there are two different solutions. Find one, and you can call it quits.

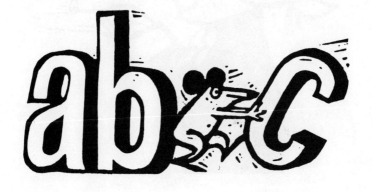

Prove that if a, b, and c are real numbers, then $a^2 + b^2 + c^2$ is never less than $ab + ac + bc$.

8 Watt Is It?

Find a base in which HEAT + WATER = STEAM.

A Matter of Expression

Solve the equation $\sqrt{x + \sqrt{x + \sqrt{x + \ldots}}} = \sqrt{x\sqrt{x\sqrt{x\ldots}}}$ where both members represent infinite expressions.

10　A Two-Scale Problem

Liquids A and B are at temperatures which are in the ratio of −3 to 1. In which scale, Fahrenheit or Celsius? Both! Find the temperatures.

The above alphametic involving Roman numerals is correct. It will still be correct if the proper Arabic numerals are substituted. Each letter denotes the same digit throughout and no 2 letters stand for the same digit. Find the unique solution.

12 Humpty Dumpty

If eggs were x¢ a dozen less, one would pay 1¢ less for x + 1 eggs than if they were x¢ a dozen more. Find x.

All Aboard! 13

A boat-owner agrees to take a group on an outing at $2.50 apiece if the number of passengers is equal to or less than his break-even point. For each person above this he reduces the fare for all passengers N cents per person. If he has on board now the number of passengers that maximizes the total collected, what is the ratio of passengers to fare per passenger?

The Drinking Bristolarians

In Bristol 90% of the citizens drink tea; 80% drink coffee; 70% drink whiskey; and 60% drink gin. No one drinks all four beverages. What percent of Bristol's citizens drink liquor?

The Four-Town Square 15 ✓

There are four towns at the corners of a square. Four motorists set out, each driving to the next (clockwise) town, and each man but the fourth going 8 mi./hr. faster than the car ahead—thus the first car travels 24 mi./hr. faster than the fourth. At the end of one hour the first and third cars are 204, and the second and fourth 212 (beeline) miles apart. How fast is the first car traveling and how far apart are the towns?

16 A Wearing Problem

A motorist rotated his five tires every 5,000 miles. At the end of 10,000 miles the original spare got slashed, and was replaced. He continued rotating every 5,000 miles, but avoided using the new tire as a spare until all five had worn equally. When the new tire first became a spare, what was the reading on the mileage gauge?

A housewife noted with dismay that brand A was 50% more expensive than C and contained 20% less weight than B. B was 50% heavier than C but cost 25% more than A. Being of an economical nature, which brand did she select?

18 A Magic Square Multiplied

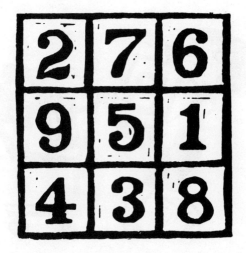

Represented above is a "magic square" in which the sum of each row, column, or main diagonal is the same. Using nine different integers, produce a "multiplicative" magic square, i.e., one in which the word "product" is substituted for "sum."

Find A and B if 7A = B and A and B together contain the ten digits 0 through 9 once and only once.

20 Think Big

Which is larger, $\sqrt{10} + \sqrt{17}$ or $\sqrt{53}$? No tables, please!

A certain 3-digit number in base 10 with no repeated digits can be expressed in base R by reversing the digits. Find the smallest value of R.

22 A Unique Number

A certain 6-digit number is a square in both the scale of 5 and the scale of 10. What is it?

What is the cube root of INVENTORY?

24 The Athletic Fraternity

All the members of a fraternity play basketball while all but one play ice hockey; yet the number of possible basketball teams (5 members) is the same as the number of possible ice-hockey teams (6 members). Assuming there are enough members to form either type of team, how many are in the fraternity?

What is the smallest base in which the two alphametics

ONE and TWO can hold?
+ ONE   + TWO
TWO   FOUR

26 Disengaging Links

What is the least number of links that must be disengaged from a 23-link chain so that any number of links from 1 to 23 can be obtained by taking one or more of the pieces?

AXIOMS, ANGLES, AND ARCS
Geometric Exercises

By the time the radius of a certain pearl has increased 1mm. the area will have increased as much (in mm.^{2}) as the volume (in mm.^{3}). If the pearl is an exact sphere, what is its radius now?

28 A Triangular Area

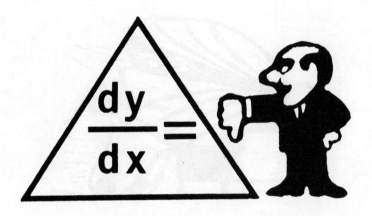

If the equal sides of an isosceles triangle are given, what length of the third side will provide maximum area? (No calculus, please.)

One side of a triangle is 10 feet longer than another and the angle between them is 60°. Two circles are drawn with these sides as diameters. One of the points of intersection of the two circles is the common vertex. How far from the third side is the other point of intersection?

30 A Swimming Problem

A kidney-shaped swimming pool is laid out by describing two tangent circles, drawing a circular arc 40 feet long tangent to both of these circles on one side and a parallel circular arc 20 feet long tangent to both of them on the other side. What is the longest (straight line) distance one can swim in this pool?

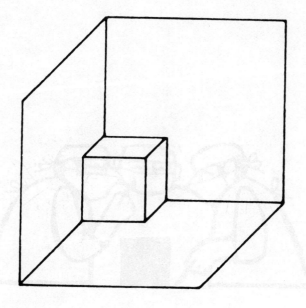

Here's a rather unusual optical illusion. How many different configurations can you "see"?

32 A Third Opinion

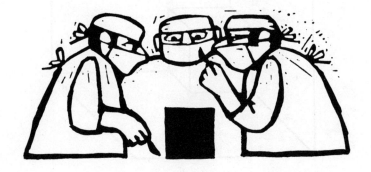

What operation can be performed three successive times on a solid cube, so that at each stage, the surface area is reduced in the same proportion as the volume?

A Precious Square 33

The price per cubic inch for platinum trays is the same as that per square inch for platinum sheets. A metal supply house has a square of platinum which will yield the same amount whether sold as a sheet, or fashioned into a tray of maximum volume with the four cut-out corners sold as sheets. How big is the square?

A Question of Quadrants

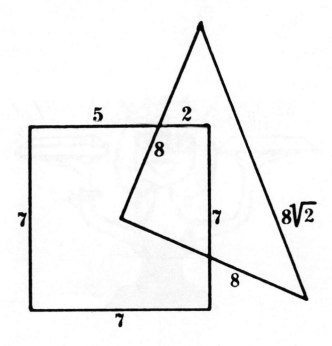

The isosceles right triangle shown above has a vertex at the center of the square. What is the area of the common quadrilateral?

There is one flag at the entrance to a racetrack and another inside the track, half a mile from the first. A jockey
notes that no matter where he is on the track, one flag
is 3 times as far away as the other. How long is the track?

36 A Horse of a Different Color

A cowboy tied his horse to a hitching post with square cross-section using a frictionless rope with a slip knot. The horse promptly pulled as far as he could in a direction straight out from the center and perpendicular to the side of the post. At what angle did the rope leave the post?

The Precocious Gauss 37

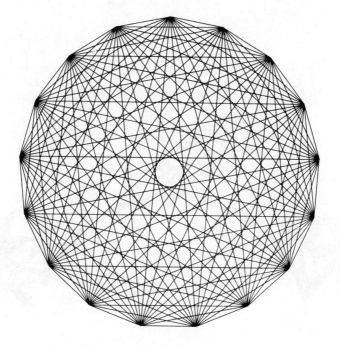

At the age of 17, Gauss proved that a regular polygon of 17 sides can be constructed with ruler and compasses. Suppose every side and every diagonal is painted either red, white, or blue. Prove at least one triangle is formed with all three sides painted the same color.

38 The Republican

Mr. X veers to the right when he walks. The curvature of his path is proportional to his latitude. He starts walking North from point A on the equator, in the area of a large level plain, and finds he is proceeding East when he is one mile north of the equator. He continues walking and arrives back at the equator at point B. What is the straight line distance from A to B?

Elliptical Billiards 39

A billiard table is in the form of an ellipse with one axis two feet longer than the other. A ball is struck from one focus and after bouncing against two cushions returns to its starting point. At the halfway point in its trip the ball is eight feet from the source. How big is the table?

40 A Yachting Angle

The pennant of the local yacht club is the usual isosceles triangle. The narrow end has an angle of 20° and the opposite side is 10 inches long. A blue stripe runs from one of the other corners to a point on the edge 10 inches from the narrow end. Determine the angle the stripe makes with the edge of the pennant.

Lazy Levy wishes to toss a snowball over a building 144 ft. x 144 ft. and 133 ft. high with the least expenditure of energy. How far away from the building should he stand? Hint: derive constraints to specify the required parabola.

42 An Inequality

Prove that each median of a triangle is shorter than the average of the 2 adjacent sides.

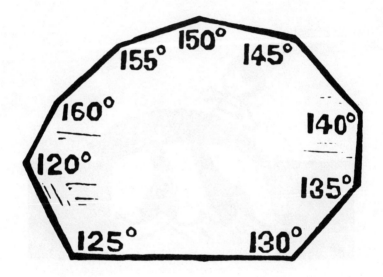

Only two polygons can have a smallest interior angle of 120° with each successive angle 5° greater than its predecessor. One is the nonagon depicted above. What is the other?

44 The Arc Bridge

A bridge across a river is in the form of an arc of a circle. A boy walking across the bridge finds that 27 feet from the shore the bridge is 9 feet above the water. He continues on to the center of the span and finds that the bridge is now 10 feet above the water. How wide is the river?

A conical drinking cup has a 12-inch rim and is 4 inches deep at the center. If creased flat, what is the vertex angle of the resulting figure?

46 A Square Problem

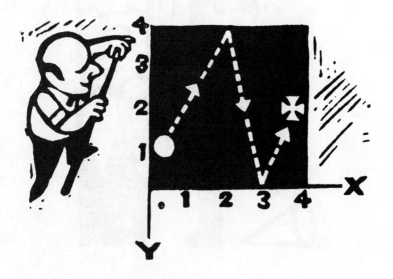

Draw the square with vertices at (0,0), (0,4), (4,4), and (4,0). A broken line is to be drawn, consisting of three segments, starting at (0,1), angling successively off the top and bottom sides of the square, and terminating at (4,2). At what points will it meet the top and bottom sides?

A hula hoop of circumference 40 inches performs one revolution about a girl with a 20-inch waist. How far has the original point of contact of the hoop traveled?

48 Diapering the Baby

A diaper is in the shape of a triangle with sides 24, 20, and 20 inches. The long side is wrapped around the baby's waist and overlapped two inches. The third point is brought up to the center of the overlap and pinned in place. The pin is to go through three thicknesses of material. What is the area in which the pin may be placed?

How can seven points be placed, no three on the same line, so that every selection of three points constitutes the vertices of an isosceles triangle?

50 Facing a Polyhedron

Prove that if all the faces of a polyhedron are triangles, the number of faces plus the number of edges is a multiple of 5.

Let c be the hypotenuse of a right triangle with legs a and b. Prove that if $x > 2$, then $a^x + b^x < c^x$.

52 Ying and Yang

A yang, ying, and yung is constructed by dividing a diameter of a circle, AB, into three parts by points C and D, then describing on one side of AB semicircles having AC and AD as diameters and on the other side of AB semicircles having BD and BC as diameters. Which is larger, the central portion or one of the outside pieces?

SOLVING IN INTEGERS
Diophantine Diversions

The equation $A^2 + B^2 + C^2 + D^2 = ABCD$ has one solution $(A,B,C,D) = (2,2,2,2)$. Find infinitely many more solutions in positive integers.

54 A Short Trip

A car accelerates uniformly from rest to 8 K mi./hr. in $\frac{K}{5}$ minutes. It continues at that speed for K minutes, then decelerates uniformly and takes another $\frac{K}{5}$ minutes to come to rest, having traveled exactly K − 1 miles altogether. The trip took an exact number of minutes. How many?

A Positive Sequence

Find an increasing sequence of positive integers N_1, $N_2 \ldots N_{12}$ in which no number is divisible by another and in which N_1 and N_{12} are minimized.

56 The Sultan's Wives

The Sultan arranged his wives in order of increasing seniority and presented each with a golden ring. Next, every 3rd wife, starting with the 2nd, was given a 2nd ring; of these every 3rd one starting with the 2nd received a 3rd ring, etc. His first and most cherished wife was the only one to receive 10 rings. How many wives had the Sultan?

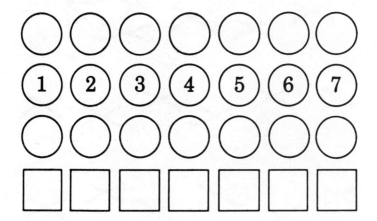

Find a permutation of the numbers one through seven with the property that when placed in both the first and third rows, the seven row totals will all be perfect squares.

58 An Infinite Expression

Let y = the infinite expression
What is the only value of
x for which x and y are
both non-zero integers?

$$x + \dfrac{x}{x + \dfrac{x}{x + \dfrac{x}{x + \dots}}}$$

Which contains more terms: the general polynomial of
tenth degree in six variables or the general polynomial
of sixth degree in ten variables?

60 The Missing Pages

Barnie Bookworm bought a thriller—found to his dismay,
Just before the denouement a fascicle astray.
Instead of counting one through ten, a standard cure
   for rages,
He totalled up the number of the missing sheaf of pages.
The total was eight thousand and six hundred fifty-six.
What were the missing pages? Try to find them just for
   kicks.

Leave six adjacent numbers of the face of a clock intact and rearrange the other six in such a way that the sum of every pair of adjacent numbers is a prime.

62 The Big Wheel

Two wheels in the same plane are mounted on shafts 13 inches apart. A belt goes around both wheels to transmit power from one to the other. The radii of the two wheels and the length of the belt not in contact with the wheels at any moment are all integers. How much larger is one wheel than the other?

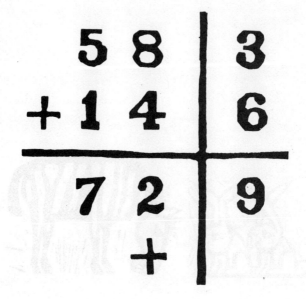

Depicted above is an example of a "two-way addition pattern" using the nine positive digits. The numbers form a correct sum as they stand or when rotated 90° to the right. Are there other such patterns, using the digits 1 through 9?

64 Shades of Diophantus

Find integers x, y, and z, such that $x^3 + y^4 = z^5$.

A Quadratic Equation

Find integers A, B, and C, positive or negative but non-zero, such that the equation $Ax^2 + Bx + C$ has roots A and B.

66 Next to One

One is the smallest integer which is simultaneously a perfect square, cube, and fifth power. What is the next smallest integer with this property?

An Unusual Number 67

What two-digit number denotes a prime in the octal and duodecimal scales as well as in the decimal scale?

The Law of Averages

Two integers were multiplied and it was noticed that d, the leftmost digit of the product, was the average of the leftmost digits of the two factors. What was d?

A Digital Product 69

Using each of the ten digits once, find two 5-digit numbers with the largest possible product.

70 Some Factorials

For what n is $\displaystyle\sum_{k=1}^{n} k!$ a square?

THE DATA SEEKERS
Problems in Logic and Deduction

True or False? 71

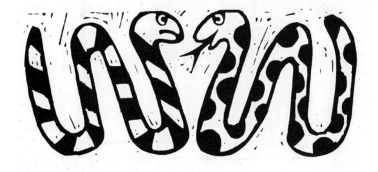

Determine the truth or falsity of the following four statements: 1. The even-numbered statements are false. 2. The odd-numbered statements are false. 3. The square-numbered statements are false. 4. Most of these four statements are false.

72 Weighing In

Any physicist will vouch that if a horse and jockey are weighed separately, their total weight will exceed the combined weight of the jockey mounted on the horse. Why?

Road signs in Puevigi consist of 4 sections, as shown, each painted a different color. It is found that 5 pints of yellow, 3 pints of blue, and 1 pint of red paint are just sufficient to comply with this restriction. What must the color scheme be?

74 A Large Number

The numbers 6,227,020,800; 6,227,028,000; and 6,227,280,000 are all large and roughly in the same ball park. But only one is equal to 13!. Find it without use of tables, desk calculators, or hard work.

The League Against Restrictive Diets, with members all over the U.S., plans a convention. Most of the members live in Chicago, so they feel that city is the logical site. The other members suggest some city representing the "weighted centroid" of the League. If the object is to minimize total distance traveled by the members of the L.A.R.D., who is right?

76 The Punchbowl

Al contributed one pint more to the punchbowl than Bob, who contributed one pint more than Carl. Don contributed none, though all shared the punch equally. Don reimbursed his friends in cash, and it was decided that Al was entitled to twice as much compensation as Bob. What proportion of money was due to Carl?

With some sharp reasoning, you ought to be able to determine the last member of the sequence for which the first 20 members are: 11, 31, 71, 91, 32, 92, 13, 73, 14, 34, 74, 35, 95, 16, 76, 17, 37, 97, 38, 98, ___?

78 A Historical Statement

Let D (x, t) denote the proposition: "Mr. x is deceived at time t." Determine the truth or falsity of the proposition: ∀ x ∃ t D (x, t) ∧ ∀ t ∃ x D (x, t) ∧ ~ [∀ x ∀ t D (x, t)].

Two astronauts are working at the same radial distance on the flat surface of their spinning cylindrical space station. "Toss me the astrowrench," says one to the other. Among the infinitude of trajectories which will successfully transfer the wrench, characterize one without writing a single equation.

80 A Parliamentary Problem

The Parliament of Puevigi plans to divide the population into ten income groups and to average the wealth between each pair of neighboring groups, starting with the two lowest, then groups two and three, ending with the top two groups. An amendment to this plan has been proposed to work from the top down. Which plan should the poorest group prefer? The richest?

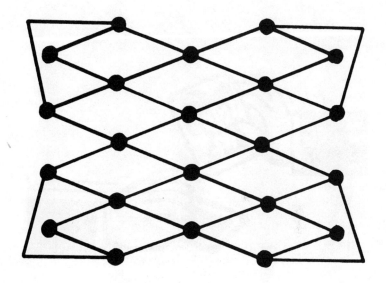

Depicted above are the 22 cities of Puevigi and their road connections. Can you devise a continuous tour which visits each city exactly once?

82 Adding Cards

Fourteen playing cards, A, 2, 3 . . . K and joker, valued 1, 2, 3 . . . 13, and 14 for the joker, are face up on a table. Two players alternately turn cards face down while keeping a running count of the sum value of the face down cards. To win, a player must, on his turn, force the sum to equal or exceed 60. Which player has the edge?

A Parental Decision

A teenager wants to go out 2 consecutive nights out of a 3-day weekend. Permission for each night is obtained (or denied) by asking either Father or Mother. Father is known to be more likely to grant permission. However, if the same parent is asked on 2 consecutive days the answers are never the same 2 days running. Whom should he ask first?

84 The Programmer's Shirts

A neat computer programmer wears a clean shirt every day. If he drops off his laundry and picks up the previous week's load every Monday night, how many shirts must he own to keep him going?

The Friendly Irish 85

Prove that at least two Irishmen have the same number of Irish friends.

86 Heads or Tails

Using a "true" coin, a random sequence of binary digits can be generated by letting, say, heads denote zero and tails, one. An operations analyst wished to obtain such a sequence, but he had only one coin, which he suspected was not true. Could he still do it?

Bowling, Anyone? 87

In a game of bowling, Jones knocked over 120 pins (the largest number possible), and Smith knocked over only 54. Assuming Smith won, what were the final scores?

88 The Brothers-in-Law

Rigorously speaking, two men are "brothers-in-law" if one is married to the full sister of the other. How many men can there be with each man a brother-in-law of every other man?

The Salesman's Tour 89

A salesman visits ten cities arranged in the form of a circle, spending a day in each. He proceeds clockwise from one city to the next, except whenever leaving the tenth city he may go to either the first or jump to the second city. How many days must elapse before his location is completely indeterminate, i.e., when he could be in any one of the ten cities?

90 Citizens of Puevigi

In the country of Puevigi, the population consists of Soothsayers, who never lie, Dissemblers, who always lie, and Diplomats, who alternately lie and tell the truth. If you meet a citizen of Puevigi, how with just two questions can you determine to which group he belongs?

Dapper Dan 91

BOB   CAL   DAN   Al

There are four boys of different ages, heights, and weights. Al, the youngest, is shorter than Bob, the heaviest, who is younger than Carl, the tallest. If no boy occupies the same rank in any two categories, how does Dan compare with the others?

92 A Tricky Sequence

Determine the next three terms of the sequence 12, 1, 1, 1, ...

MINDING YOUR P's AND Q's
Probability Posers

One of a pair of dice is loaded so that the chance of a 1 turning up is ⅕, the other faces being equally likely. Its mate is loaded so that the chance of a 6 turning up is ⅕, the other faces being equally likely. How much does this loading increase the probability of throwing a 7 with the two dice?

94 • The Weather Report

The local weather forecaster says "no rain" and his record is ⅔ accuracy of prediction. But the Federal Meteorological Service predicts rain and *their* record is ¾. *A priori* it's as likely as not to rain. What is the chance of rain?

A Born Sucker 95

A sharp operator makes the following deal. A player is to toss a coin and receive $1, 4, 9, \ldots n^2$ dollars if the first head comes up on the first, second, third, $\ldots$ n-th toss. The sucker pays ten dollars for this. How much can the operator expect to make if this is repeated a great many times?

96 1984 World Series

In 1984, the World Series will begin in the stadium of the National League pennant winner. Assume the contenders are evenly matched. What is the probability that the series will end where it began?

In a carnival game 5 balls are tossed into a square box divided into 4 square cells, with baffles to insure that every ball has an equal chance of going in any cell. The player pays $1 and receives $1 for every cell which is empty after the 5 balls are thrown. How much does the operator expect to make per game?

98 Wednesday's Child

How many people would you expect to meet before you met one who was born on a Wednesday?

Venusian batfish come in *three* sexes, which are indistinguishable (except by Venusian batfish). How many live specimens must our astronauts bring home in order for the odds to favor the presence of a "mated triple" with its promise of more little batfish to come?

100 Another Carnival Game

In a carnival game, 12 white balls and 3 black balls are put in an opaque bottle, shaken up, and drawn out one at a time. The player gets 25 cents for each white ball which emerges before the first black ball. If he pays one dollar to play, how much can he expect to win (or lose) on each game?

The squares on a checkerboard are numbered in random fashion with the numbers 1, 2, . . . , 64. Find the probability that a "saddle square" exists (simultaneously a row minimum and a column maximum).

102 Max and Min's Vacation

Max and his wife Min each toss a pair of dice to determine where they will spend their vacation. If either of Min's dice displays the same number of spots as either of Max's, she wins and they go to Bermuda. Otherwise, they go to Yellowstone. What is the chance they'll see "Old Faithful" this year?

There are four volumes of an encyclopedia on a shelf, each volume containing 300 pages (that is, numbered 1 to 600), but these have been placed on the shelf in random order. A bookworm starts at the first page of Vol. 1 and eats his way through to the last page of Vol. 4. What is the expected number of pages (excluding covers) he has eaten through?

104 The Olive Stuffer

An amphora contains black and green olives. An olive stuffer wishes to estimate which type is more abundant by sampling two olives at random. To optimize his estimate, should he sample with or without replacement?

Six men decide to play Russian roulette with a six-gun loaded with one cartridge. They draw for position, and, afterwards, the sixth man casually suggests that, instead of letting the chamber rotate in sequence, each man spin the chamber before shooting. How would this improve his chances?

106 The Piggy Bank

If a coin were randomly shaken out of a certain piggy bank, its expected value would be 15 cents. If a dime had been added, the expected value would have been only 14 cents. What are the contents of the bank?

A roulette player made 5 straight even-money bets on the red. Starting with 32 chips, he bet half his current holdings each time. Red came up 3 times, black twice. In what order would he want his 3 wins to come to maximize his profit? How much would his profit be?

108 A Pat Hand

A long-shot poker player draws two cards to the five and six of diamonds and the joker. What are his chances of coming up with a pat hand (straight or flush)?

Puevigian Craps 109

In Puevigi, the game of craps is played with a referee calling the point by adding together the six faces (three on each die) visible from his vantage point. What is the probability of making 16 the hard way? (That is, by throwing two eights.)

110 **Bridge Partners**

In a hand of Bridge, which is the more likely event: you and your partner have all 13 cards in one suit, or both of you are void in the same suit?

If 2 marbles are removed at random from a bag containing black and white marbles, the chance that they are both white is ⅓. If 3 are removed at random, the chance that they all are white is ⅙. How many marbles are there of each color?

112 Who's Safe?

An expert gives team A only a 40% chance to win the World Series. Basing his calculation on this a gambler offers 6 to 5 odds on team B to win the first game. Is his judgment sound?

An Unbalanced Coin 113

A coin is so unbalanced that you are as likely to get two heads in two successive throws as you are to get tails in one. What is the probability of getting heads in a single throw?

114 **Dart Tic-Tac-Toe**

Three dart players threw simultaneously at a tic-tac-toe board, each hitting a different square. What is the probability that the three hits constituted a win at tic-tac-toe?

Martian coins are 3-sided (heads, tails, and torsos), each side coming up with equal probability. Three Martians decided to go odd-man-out to determine who pays a dinner check. (If two coins come up the same and one different, the owner of the latter coin foots the bill.) What is the expected number of throws needed in order to determine a loser?

NOW YOU SEE IT
Insight Puzzles

Besides direction, what property is shared by Santa's helpers at the North Pole, the Northwest Passage, and that hundredth root of unity which is northernmost in the Argand plane?

117 O'Toole's Quatrain

In a mystic mood Archimedes O'Toole penned the quatrain: Perfection lies in $\binom{4}{2}$ and $\binom{8}{2}/\binom{3}{2} + \binom{5}{2}$ should ne'er be seated at a feast / And *Revelations* clearly indicate / The nature and the true $\binom{37}{2}$. Translate into plain English with rhyme and perfect scansion in iambic pentameter.

There are at least two ways of representing 20, using three 3's and standard mathematical symbols. Find one.

119 **The Nine Planets**

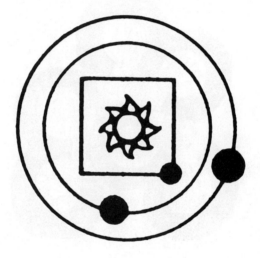

Which of the nine planets' ecliptics is most eccentric?

"The greater the mass, the faster the object will fall," said Aristotle. Prove him wrong without equations and without dropping objects from the Tower of Pisa.

X 121 **Deciphering a Code**

A simple substitution cipher message was worked out on a blackboard and accidentally erased. A few fragments remain, however. The word G Q K X Y J has escaped erasure with X identified as R and Y as B. Also the word P K Z X D V can be made out with Z identified as L. The only other legible word is K V J Z D C. What word does this represent?

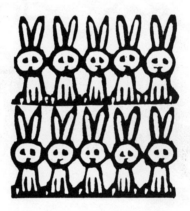

What does a mule have in common with an out-of-order xerox machine?

123 A Sum of Squares

For x, y, and z real numbers, solve the equation
$3x^2 + y^2 + z^2 = 2x(y + z)$.

By the same token that POLYMER is a good "telepho-mnemonic" for an organic chemist whose number is SNowden 59637, find two good ones for a geophysicist whose number is VErnon 62567 and a surfer whose number is WHitney 73688.

125 Friday the 13th

What is the last year which had no "Friday the 13ths"?

What do the following have in common: The Greenwich Meridian, a fine roast rib of beef, television time from 7 to 10 P.M., and a positive integer n which divides the number $(n-1)! + 1$?

127 A Recursive Sequence

Consider the sequence $0, 1, 2, 7, 20, 61, \ldots$ in which $A_{n+2} = 3A_n + 2A_{n+1}$. Assuming the ratio of successive terms approaches a limit r, compute r.

A number of 5 x 8 cards have been divided into 1-inch squares numbered 1 to 40. It is desired to use these for window cards with exactly six of the interior 18 squares cut out. How many different cards can be made?

129 Complete the Jig-Saw

A jig-saw puzzle contains 100 pieces. A "move" consists of connecting two clusters (including "clusters" of just one piece). What is the minimum number of moves required to complete the puzzle?

There are three errers in the statement of this problem. You must detect all of them to recieve full credit.

131 Playing Connecto

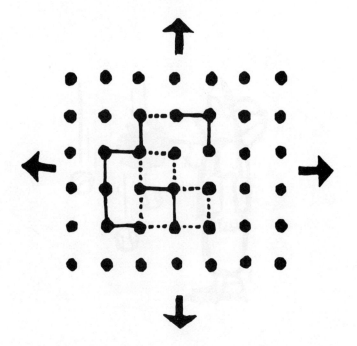

In the game of "connecto," 2 players alternate in joining adjacent points, horizontally or vertically, on an infinite rectangular lattice, one using solid lines for his connections, the other, dashes. The winner is the first to enclose a region of any shape by a boundary composed of his symbol only. (The player with the dashes has won above.) Is the 2nd player doomed to defeat?

A novice librarian shelved a twelve-volume set of ency-clopedias in the following order from left to right. Volumes 8, 11, 5, 4, 9, 1, 7, 6, 10, 3, 12, and 2. Using her system, where will the annual supplement, Volume 13, go?

An International Problem

"Four" in English, "cinco" in Spanish, and "ni" and "san" in Japanese share an interesting property. What is it?

The set A contains the integers 0, 4, 5, 9, 11, 12, 13, 14, 19, ... The set B contains 1, 2, 3, 6, 7, 8, 10, 15, 16, 17, 18, ... Place 20 and 21 in their proper sets.

√ 135 **An Unusual Sharing**

What property is common to sports of rowing and tug-of-war, the planet Uranus, and a clock whose hands move at the correct rate but which gives the right time only 4 times daily?

In a certain code used in high-level communication in Puevigi, the two permutations of the nine positive digits 692547318 and 768415932 are code equivalents, respectively, of the words INTERVENE and EXTROVERT. Break the code and decipher 895173246.

137 **Another Odd Sharing**

What property is common to Arctic penguins, peacock eggs, the Hungarian Merchant Marine, the University of Chicago football team, 19-point cribbage hands, and the solution set of the equation $e^{e^x} = 1$?

Post-Apollo mission planners have considered the merits of orbiting synchronous (orbital period matching the rotational period of the primary) lunar satellites. At approximately what altitude with respect to the moon would such a satellite orbit?

139 Jack's Beanstalk

of (original H + ½ original H)

Very few people are aware of the growth pattern of Jack's beanstalk. On the first day it increased its height by ½, on the second day by ⅓, on the third day by ¼, and so on. How long did it take to achieve its maximum height (100 times its original height)?

PERMUTATIONS, PARTITIONS, AND PRIMES
Assorted Number Theory Problems

A Cross-Number Problem 140 ✓

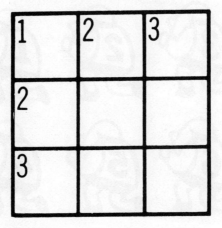

Find the unique solution to this cross-number puzzle.
Across: 1. A Fibonacci number; 2. A square; 3. A perfect number. Down: 1. A square; 2. A cube; 3. A number.

✓ 141 A Digital Progression

→ 6!

If all 720 permutations of the digits 1 through 6 are arranged in numerical order, what is the 417th term?

$$\frac{8712}{2178} = 4 \qquad \frac{9801}{1089} = 9$$

If an integer is a factor of its reversal, then the ratio is a square. Prove it.

143 The Quitter

Using a desk calculator, a student was asked to obtain the *complete* factorization of 24,949,501. Dividing by successively increasing primes, he found the smallest prime divisor to be 499 with quotient 49,999. At this point, he quit. Why didn't he carry the factorization to completion?

What is the smallest positive integer which, when divided by any N in the range 2, 3, ..., 10, leaves a remainder of N–1?

145 Prime Pairs

$$71 \times 73 = 5183$$
$$5 + 1 + 8 + 3 = 17$$
$$1 + 7 = \underline{\underline{8}}$$

Prove that the digital sum of the product of any prime pair (except 3 and 5) is 8.

The Seance 146

Some couples plan to hold seances around a round table. Dropping the usual requirement that men and women alternate, they find the number of possible seating arrangements is increased tenfold. How many couples are there?

147 Numerical Links

A chain of numbers can be constructed by starting with any 2 numbers, adding them to produce a 3rd, adding the 2nd and 3rd to produce a 4th, etc. Any number can be obtained by means of such a "Fibonoid" chain if the starting values are properly chosen. If one wishes to produce the number 1,000,000 by the longest possible chain of positive integers, with what 2 must he start?

Show, with a simple example, that an irrational number raised to an irrational power need not be irrational.

149 Non-Primes

Prove that neither 999,919 nor 1,000,343 is prime.

A Multiple Marriage

There are three families, each with two sons and two daughters. In how many ways can all these young people be married?

151 The Wrestling Octopi

Two octopi indulged in a friendly tentacle-to-tentacle wrestling match. Each managed to pin 4 of his opponent's tentacles with 4 of his own. In how many ways was this possible?

1,2,2,3,3,3,4,4,4,4,

What is the millionth term of the sequence 1, 2, 2, 3, 3, 3, 4, 4, 4, 4, . . . in which each positive integer n occurs in blocks of n terms?

153 A Prime Proof

Prove that whenever P and $P^2 + 2$ are both prime, $P^2 + 4$ is also prime.

Six boys on a hockey team pick a captain by forming a circle and counting out until only one remains. Joe is given the option of deciding what number to count by. If he is second in the original counting order what number should he choose?

155 A Mirror Reflection

In the arithmetic of Puevigi, 14 is a factor of 41. What is the base of the number system?

Super-Dominoes 156

A game of super-dominoes is played with pieces divided into three cells instead of the usual two, containing all combinations from triple blank to triple six, with no duplications. For example the set does not include both 1 2 3 and 3 2 1 since these are merely reversals of each other. (But, it does contain 1 3 2.) How many pieces are there in a set?

157 **One Solution**

Find the only number consisting of five different digits
which is a factor of its reversal.

No factorial can end in five zeros. What is the next small-est number of zeros in which a factorial can *not* end?

1. Solving the inequalities simultaneously, we find that $56\frac{1}{4} > N > 53\frac{1}{3}$. Knowing that $N = 54, 55$, or 56, the other inequalities lead to the unique solution: $P = 26$, $E = 19$, $N = 55$. $\quad N > 2P \ \ \& \ \ 3E > 2P \rightarrow \ N+E > \frac{8}{3}P \rightarrow \ 27.27 > P \ etc.$

2. If Pete has twice as many as Luke after an odd number of minutes and this ratio is increased to 7:3 in 5 minutes, they each must have started with 126 potatoes (100:50 after 51 minutes, 98:42 after 56 minutes). Likewise, if Pete has twice as many as Luke after an even number of minutes they must have started with 100 potatoes each (80:40 after 40 minutes, 77:33 after 45 minutes). In the first case the ratio will never be 3:1. In the second case this occurs after another 5 minutes, at which time they have 75 and 25 potatoes left.

3. The number of solutions of a set of polynomial equations is the product of their degrees. Since hyperbolas are of 2nd degree, the solutions to a pair of hyperbolic equations cannot exceed 4. Thus two hyperbolas can intersect in no more than 4 points.

4. Since $(H + 10A) (A + 10H) = 1001 \ T + 100 \ H + 10A$, $1001 \ T = (A + 10H) (H + 10A - 10)$. The factors of 1001, namely 7, 11, and 13, must divide the right member, and only the value $T = 6$ permits an integral solution. Hence THAT is 6786.

5. The only orthonym in English is TWENTY NINE. Polyglots are invited to find orthonyms in other languages. $\quad\checkmark\ Note: A, N, \textit{or } I = 4,3,2, \textit{or } 1$
$\qquad\qquad\qquad\qquad\qquad\qquad\qquad\qquad\qquad O, U, R \textit{ or } E = 0$

6. (1) (26) (345) = 8970 and (2) (14) (307) = 8596.

7. This follows directly from the inequality $(a - b)^2 + (a - c)^2 + (b - c)^2 \geqq 0$.

8. Since $R \pm M$, $T \pm 0$. Hence the 3rd column implies that $T = B - 1$, where $B =$ the base. However, in order that a carry-over from the 2nd column occur, $E = B - 1$ also. This contradiction proves that there is no base in which HEAT + WATER = STEAM.

9. Let each expression $= y$. Squaring both sides, $y^2 = x + y = xy$. Hence $y = x$, $2x = x^2$, and $x = 0$ or 2.

10. Let A and $B = -3A$ be Celsius temperatures. It will quickly be seen that, in switching to the Fahrenheit scale, the ratio is reversed so that $\frac{9}{5}A + 32 = -3$ $(-\frac{27}{5} A + 32)$ and $A = -\frac{80°}{3}$ C or 48°F while $B = \frac{80}{9}$ C or -16°F.

11. C cannot be 4 since X and L would both be 2. Hence $C = 9$ and $X = 3$, and the unique solution: $453 + 485 = 938$ is obtained.

12. Let $y =$ present price per dozen. Then if the price were x cents per dozen less, $x + 1$ eggs would cost $1/12 (y - x) (x + 1)$. If the price were x cents per dozen more, $x + 1$ eggs would cost $1/12 (y + x) (x + 1)$. Thus $(y + x) (x + 1) - (y - x) (x + 1) = 12$, giving $x(x + 1) = 6$, from which $x = 2$.

13. Let $A =$ number of passengers required to break even and $A + x$ the actual number on board. Then $(A + x) (250 - N x)$ will be collected. This will be a maximum when $x = \dfrac{250 - AN}{2N}$. Then the number of passengers will be $A + \dfrac{250 - AN}{2N}$ or $\dfrac{AN + 250}{2N}$ each paying $250 - \dfrac{250 - AN}{2}$ or $\dfrac{250 + AN}{2}$. Therefore the fare per passenger will be N times the number of passengers.

14. Let T denote the set of citizens who drink tea and T^1 the ones who don't, and so forth. Then T^1 contains 10% of Bristol's citizens; C^1, 20%; W^1, 30%; and G^1, 40%. Since no one drinks all four beverages, the union of T^1, C^1, W^1, and G^1 contains 100% of the citizens, implying that these four sets are disjoint in pairs. This means that every citizen partakes of three of the four beverages. Hence 100% drink liquor.

15. If X is the distance between two neighboring towns and R the rate of the 4th car, we have $X^2 + [X - (2 \ R + 32)]^2 = 204^2$ and $X^2 + [X - (2 \ R + 16)]^2 = 212^2$, from which $X = 2R + 128$ and substituting this in either equation yields $R = 26$ or $R = -154$. This latter must be rejected, so that the first car traveled 50 mi./hr. and the distance between neighboring towns is $2 \times 26 + 128$ or 180 miles.

16. 45,000 miles, at which time all five tires had had 35,000 miles of wear.

17. A and B are of equal value, while C has a 20% economy edge over both.

18. Using the rule that powers multiply by adding their exponents, a multiplicative magic square is easily obtained from the given square by substituting 2^n (or k^n where $k > 1$) for n in each block.

19. Both A and B must be 5-digit numbers, and A must be less than 14286. A can end only in 2, 4, 6, 7, 8, or 9. Likewise there are only 27 2-digit endings for A. These in turn place restrictions on the hundreds digit, etc., so that it is not too difficult to find the only admissible values of A and B. $7 \times 14076 = 98532$.

20. $(\sqrt{10} + \sqrt{17})^2 = 10 + 2\sqrt{170} + 17 > 27 + 2\sqrt{169} = 53$. Hence, $\sqrt{10} + \sqrt{17} > \sqrt{53}$.

21. If we call the digits A, B, and C, we have $A + 10B + 100C = C + RB + R^2A$ or $99C = (R^2 - 1) A + (R - 10) B$. R must be at least 3 in order to produce three distinct digits. Values of R from 3 to 13 yield no solution in integers A, B, C, all distinct and less than R (or 10, whichever is smaller). But $R = 14$ yields the solution $A = 4$, $B = 3$, $C = 8$. Therefore $R = 14$. $834_{10} = 438_{14}$.

22. Squares in the scale of 5 can end only in 0, 1, or 4. In the scale of 10, a 0 must be preceded by a 0, and 1 or 4 must be preceded by an even number. These even numbers in the penultimate position must be 0, 2, or 4, since 6 and 8 would be impossible in the scale of 5. Proceeding in this way, imposing similar restrictions on the other digits, we find 232324 as the only number which is a square in both bases, $232324 = 332^2$ in the scale of 5 and $= 482^2$ in the scale of 10.

23. Restrictions on the final digits of cubes (e.g., if the units digit is 2 or 6 the tens digit must be odd and if 4 or 8 the tens digit must be even, etc.) allow us to cut the number of possibilities for R and Y to manageable size. These in turn determine the last two digits of the cube root and since this lies between 465 and 999 (in order to produce a 9-digit number when cubed) we can try all the possibilities and reject those which do not have only the fifth and eighth digits the same. We find $317,214,568 = (682)^3$ is the only admissible value. Substituting the letter equivalents of 682, the cube root of INVENTORY is RYE.

24. Let the fraternity have x members. Then $\binom{x}{5} = \binom{x-1}{6}$, leading to a quadratic equation with roots $x = 2$ or 15. Only the latter meets the conditions of the problem. Thus the fraternity had 15 members and could field 3,003 teams of either type.

25. Obviously $F = 1$. Also $2(0) + 1 = T$ and either $2T = B + 0$ or $2T + 1 = B + 0$ where B is the base. Thus $B = 3(0) + 2$ or $3(0) + 3$. The base is at least 8 since there are 8 different letters. 8, 9, 11, and 12 are readily eliminated and 10 and 13 are not of the required form mod 3. The smallest possible base is 14 with $0 = 4$, $N = 10$, $E = 2$, $T = 9$, $W = 6$, $F = 1$, $U = 12$, and $R = 8$.

26. Two. The 4th and the 11th.

27. We have $4\pi(r + 1)^2 - 4\pi r^2 = \frac{4\pi}{3}(r + 1)^3 - \frac{4\pi}{3} r^3$ from which $3r^2 - 3r - 2 = 0$. $r = \frac{1}{2} + \frac{1}{6} \sqrt{33} \cong 1.457$ mm.

28. Picture one of the equal sides as the base and let the other side swing in a semicircle. Since the base is fixed, the area is largest when the altitude is longest, i.e., when the two equal sides are perpendicular. Hence the third side will be $\sqrt{2}$ times the length of one of the equal sides.

29. At zero distance! Regardless of the angles or lengths of the sides, if a line is drawn connecting the two points of intersection, it will be perpendicular to the third side. (Recall that an angle inscribed in a semicircle is a right angle.) Hence the point of intersection will lie on the third side.

30. The longest distance will be along the line joining the centers of the two circles, hence will be twice the diameter. The two circular arcs must be tangent at the ends of diameters. If these diameters, when extended, meet at an angle of 2 Θ, $\sin \Theta = \dfrac{20-10}{20+10}$ so that $\Theta = \arcsin \frac{1}{3}$. The diameter is $\dfrac{20}{2\Theta}$; therefore the required distance is $\dfrac{40}{2\Theta}$ or approximately 58¾ feet.

31. 1. A little cube nestled in the corner of a big one. 2. A big cube with a cubical chunk removed from one corner. 3. Two cubes meeting externally at a corner. If you perceived all 3, congratulations! If you saw *any other* configurations, what are they??

32. Turning! (as on a lathe). A cube with side D can be turned down to a cylinder of diameter D. This can be turned down about an axis at right angles to the first, and the resulting solid further turned down about the axis normal to the other two. Straightforward (if slightly tedious) integration gives the results $S/6D^2 = V/D^3 = \pi/4, 2/3, 2 - \sqrt{2}$ for the three solids.

33. Maximum volume is obtained when the 4 cut-out squares have sides 1/6 those of the original square, in which case $V = \dfrac{2}{27} S^3$. Hence the tray plus remnants will sell for $\dfrac{2}{27} S^3 + \dfrac{S^2}{9}$ units, while the sheet will sell for S^2 units. Equating these prices, S = exactly one foot.

34. Rotating the Δ about the square's center does not change the common area; what is lost in one quadrant is added to an adjacent quadrant. Therefore, rotate so that the two legs of the Δ are flush with the square's diagonals. Then the common area is readily seen to be ¼ that of the square or 12.25.

35. In order for any point on the track to be 3 times as far from one flag as the other, the track must be circular, with diameter ¾ the distance between the flags. The track must, therefore, have diameter 1980 ft., so that its circumference is 1980 π ft. or about 9.42 furlongs.

36. Interestingly, the angle is independent of the lengths of the rope and the side of the post. By symmetry, the three tensions at the point of the slip knot are equal in magnitude and uniformly separated by angles of 120° at the time of equilibrium. Hence the required angle is 30°. An astute reader pointed out that with a frictionless rope a slip knot will not hold. If you recognized this, give yourself double credit.

37. From any vertex P at least 6 lines of the same color (say red) emanate, joining P say to A, B, C, D, E, and F. If any connection among these is red, a red Δ is formed. If not, 3 of the lines AB, AC, AD, AE, and AF are the same color (say the first three are white). Then if BC, BD, or CD is white, a white Δ is formed with vertex at A. Otherwise Δ BCD is blue!

38. A radius of length l/y with one end moving along the x axis (equator) and the other end at height y (latitude) generates a curve in which K = 2y, based on the equation $dx/dy = \dfrac{y^2}{\sqrt{1-y^4}}$. If the radius makes angle Θ with the x axis, $y^2 = \sin \Theta$, and the equation transforms to $x = \displaystyle\int_0^{\pi/2} \dfrac{\sqrt{\sin \Theta}\, d\Theta}{2}$ for each quadrant. Thus $\overline{AB} = 2x = $ a trifle less than 1.2 miles.

39. At the halfway point the ball is at the other focus. Let A and A + 1 be the lengths of the semi-axes; then the distance between the foci will be 2 $\sqrt{(A+1)^2 - A^2}$. If this = 8, A = 15/2. The table is, therefore, an ellipse with axes of 15 and 17 feet.

40. Let BC be the side opposite the 20° angle and D the point 10″ from A on side AB. Construct triangle ADE congruent to ABC with ED ∥ BC. Join EC. Then triangle AEC is equilateral and angle DEC = 40°. Triangle EDC is isosceles and angle EDC is 70°. Thus the stripe makes an angle of 150° (or its supplement) with the edge.

41. The potential energy of any particle at roof height h is mgh. Since total energy is conserved along any parabola, the least energy parabola may be viewed as requiring least kinetic energy to clear the roof from height h. The required parabola thus forms a 45° angle with each roof edge, and the distance from the base is found to be

$$\sqrt{144\left(133 + \frac{144}{4}\right)} - \frac{144}{2} = 84 \text{ ft.}$$

42. Reflect the triangle through the opposite side. The problem now reduces to proving a diagonal of the resulting parallelogram is shorter than the sum of 2 adjacent sides. This follows from the triangle inequality.

43. The sum of the interior angles of an n-gon is 180 (n − 2) degrees. The required n-gon will have an angle sum of $120n + \frac{n(n-1)}{2} \cdot 5$ degrees. Equating the 2 expressions, n = 9 or 16. The other polygon is, therefore, the hexadecagon. If you noted that one angle was a "straight angle" and you correctly identified the required polygon as a "pentadecagon" (15-sided polygon), give yourself a bonus.

44. Let R be the radius of the circle and 2 W the width of the river. Then $W^2 + (R - 10)^2 = R^2$ and $(W - 27)^2 + (R - 1)^2 = R^2$. Then $W^2 = 20 R - 100$ and $3 W - R = 35$, from which W = 20, or W = 40. W = 20 must be rejected since 27 feet from the shore must be less than halfway across. Hence W = 40 and the river is 80 feet wide.

45. The slant height in inches is $\sqrt{16 + \left(\frac{6}{\pi}\right)^2} = \frac{2}{\pi}\sqrt{4\pi^2 + 9}$. The creased figure will be a sector of a circle with arc length = 6, and radius = $\frac{2}{\pi}\sqrt{4\pi^2 + 9}$. The angle of such sector is $3\pi/\sqrt{4\pi^2 + 9}$ or 77° 33′ approximately.

46. Draw 2 additional 4 × 4 squares atop the one already drawn, and connect the points (0,1) and (4,10) with a straight line. Using the principle of reflection, the desired points are found to be (4/3,4) and (28/9,0).

47. If the hoop is thought of as stationary with the girl rotating, the original point of contact traverses the diameter of the hoop twice, or a distance of 80/π inches.

48. The required area will be a diamond-shaped figure composed of two triangles with a common base, each triangle having sides 1, 5/6, and 5/6 inches. The area of each is 1/3, so that the total area in which the pin may be placed is 2/3 sq. in.

49. Place five at the vertices of a regular pentagon, the sixth at the center of the pentagon, and the seventh above the center at a distance equal to the radius of the pentagon.

50. Associate each of the E edges with one of the two faces on which it lies; each of the F faces then has an average of 1½ edges associated with it. Then $F + E = \frac{3}{2}F = \frac{5}{2}F$. Since F + E is an integer, F must be even, and $F + E = 5\left(\frac{F}{2}\right)$ is a multiple of 5.

51. $a^x + b^x = a^2 a^{x-2} + b^2 b^{x-2} < a^2 c^{x-2} + b^2 c^{x-2} = (a^2 + b^2)c^{x-2} = c^2 c^{x-2} = c^x$.

52. All three are the same size, each being equal to $\frac{1}{3}\pi R^2$, where R is the radius of the circle.

53. By substitution it can be verified that if (A, B, C, D) is a solution, then (BCD—A, B, C, D) is also a solution. This gives rise to an infinitude of solutions: (2, 2, 2, 2), (6, 2, 2, 2), (6, 22, 2, 2), etc.

54. The car can be assumed to travel 4 K mi./hr. throughout the acceleration and deceleration periods, thus traveling $K^2/75$ miles at each end of the trip. In between it goes 8 K mi./hr. for K minutes, thus going $2K^2/15$ miles in the middle. Altogether it travels $(2K^2/75) + (2K^2/15)$ miles. If this is equal to $K - 1, 4K^2 - 25K + 25 = 0$, from which $K = 5$ or $5/4$. Since the number of minutes is an integer, K must be 5, and the trip took 7 minutes.

55. 4, 6, 9, 10, 11, 13, 14, 15, 17, 19, 21, and 23.

56. Number the wives in base 3, thus: 1, 2, 10, 11, 12, 20, . . . , and note that if the last digit is not 2, the wife has only one ring. If the last 2 digits are 02 or 22, she has two rings; if the last 3 digits are 012 or 212, she has three, etc. Hence the wife with ten rings had position 111111112 (base 3) and the sultan had 9,842 wives (roughly 1 a day for 27 years).

57. The row totals are all either 4, 9, or 16. But since the total of the 21 circles is $3(28) = 84$, and no partition of 84 into 7 numbers of the form 4, 9, or 16 can contain a 4 (readily proven), there are four 9's and three 16's. Obviously the even rows are the ones which total 16, and the unique sequence 4 7 3 6 2 5 1 is obtained.

58. $y = x + x/y$. Solving for x, $x = y^2/(y + 1)$, implying $y + 1$ is a divisor of y^2. Since $y + 1$ is also a divisor of $y^2 - 1$, it is a divisor of their difference, 1. Hence $y + 1 = \pm 1$. Rejecting the positive sign which makes $y = 0$, the unique solution $x = -4$, $y = -2$ is obtained.

59. The general polynomial of nth degree in k variables has $\binom{n + k}{n}$ terms. Since, however, $\binom{n + k}{n} = \binom{k + n}{k}$, there is symmetry between degree and number of variables. In the specific case considered the number of terms is 8,008 in both instances.

60. The number of missing pages, p, is obviously even, while n, the first missing page number, is odd (since it is a right-hand page). The number of the last page is $n + p - 1$, and the total of the missing page numbers is $\dfrac{(n + p - 1)(n + p)}{2} - \dfrac{(n - 1)(n)}{2} = \dfrac{p}{2}$ $(2n + p - 1) = 8656$ or $p(2n + p - 1) = (32)(541)$ with the first factor even, the second odd. Hence $p = 32$, $n = 255$ and pp. 255–286 are missing.

61. 1, 2, 3, 4, 7, 10, 9, 8, 5, 6, 11, 12 is one possibility. The only other one is 1, 2, 3, 4, 9, 10, 7, 6, 5, 8, 11, 12.

62. Let the radius of the smaller wheel be A and of the larger wheel B. Then the length of the belt not in contact with the wheels is $2\sqrt{169 - (B - A)^2}$. For this to be integral, $(B - A)^2$ must be 25 or 144. If one wheel were 12 in. larger in radius than the other, the wheels would overlap and could not be in the same plane. Therefore, one wheel is 5 in. larger in radius than the other.

63. With some trial and deduction it can be shown that there is only one other such pattern, viz., $482 + 157 = 639$.

64. Assume $x = a^8$, $y = b^6$, and $z = c^5$. Then $a^{24} + b^{24} = c^{25}$ or $(a/c)^{24} + (b/c)^{24} = c$. Now let $a/c = m$ and $b/c = n$. Then $c = m^{24} + n^{24}$, $a = m(m^{24} + n^{24})$, and $b = n(m^{24} + n^{24})$. This yields the two-parameter solution $x = m^8(m^{24} + n^{24})^8$; $y = n^6(m^{24} + n^{24})^6$; $z = (m^{24} + n^{24})^5$ for arbitrary integers m and n.

65. We have $(x - A)(x - B) = 0$ and multiplying by A, $Ax^2 - A(A + B)x + A^2B = 0$. Equating the coefficients of x, $B = -A(A + B)$ or $B = -A^2/(A + 1)$. Since $A + 1$ divides A^2, $A(A + 1) - A^2 = A$ is also a multiple of $A + 1$. Moreover $(A + 1) - A = 1$ is a multiple of $A + 1$. Hence $A + 1 = \pm 1$. Since $A \neq 0$, $A = -2$, $B = 4$, and $C = 16$.

66. In the factorization of a perfect nth power, each prime factor has an exponent divisible by n. Consequently, if a number is a square, cube, and a fifth power, every prime factor has an exponent divisible by LCM $(2, 3, 5) = 30$. Thus the number is a perfect 30th power, and the second smallest such number is 2^{30}.

67. 37. The digits 8 and 9 are ruled out since the number is meaningful in the octal scale. The second digit cannot be 0, 2, 4, 5, or 6, since such a number would be composite in the decimal scale. Nor can it be 3, since the number would then be a multiple of 3 in base 12. Hence the second digit is 1 or 7, and the candidates are 11, 31, 41, 61, 71, 17, 37, 47, or 67. All of these except 37 are composite in the octal scale.

68. By making a table, the solver can convince himself that d cannot be properly between the leftmost digits of the two factors. Hence all three numbers have the same leftmost digit d, which must, therefore, be 1, 8, or 9.

69. Using two principles, namely (1) the largest digits go to the left and (2) the product of two numbers whose sum is constant is maximized by making their difference as small as possible, the solution 96,420 and 87,531 is obtained.

70. Only for n = 1 or 3. Otherwise, the terminal digit of Σ is 3, while a square must end in 0, 1, 4, 5, 6, or 9.

71. Starting with an assumption regarding the truth or falsity of any of the four statements, one is invariably led to a contradiction. The statements as a group are, therefore, not "meaningful" in our two-valued logic.

72. Because the jockey's centroid, when mounted, is farther from that of the earth.

73. Each pint covers 72/9 = 8 sq. ft. Mix 2¼ pints (= 18 sq. ft.) of yellow with a similar amount of blue to make 4½ pints (= 36 sq. ft.) of green. This leaves just enough blue for the innermost ring. The position of the other colors follows.

74. 13! = 1·2·3·4·5 . . . *10* . . . 13. Since five is a factor of multiplicity two, 13! must end in *two* zeros. The first number is, therefore, the right one. Alternate solution: the 2nd and 3rd numbers are not divisible by 7.

75. Assume the site is not Chicago. Pair each non-Chicagoan with a Chicagoan. Moving the site to Chicago will not increase the total mileage. In fact, since there are unpaired Chicagoans, it will decrease it. Hence Chicago is the proper site, regardless of the geographic distribution of the other members.

76. Since Al was paid twice as much as Bob, his contribution minus his consumption was twice that of Bob, i.e., 2 pints to 1. Thus everyone drank 3 pints (5, 4, and 3 from Al, Bob, and Carl) and Carl, who drank all he contributed, was paid nothing.

77. By noticing the progression of the second digits, you might have deduced that this is the sequence of reversals of 2-digit primes in ascending order. The last member is 79.

78. True, at least if you agree with Abraham Lincoln that ". . . you can fool all of the people some of the time and some of the people all of the time, but you can't fool all of the people all of the time."

79. Neither a line-of-sight toss nor a simple release will work. However, if the thrower imparts to the wrench a velocity equal to his own tangential velocity and opposite in direction, the wrench will remain stationary above the spinning satellite and will presently be met by the other astronaut.

80. Both the poorest and the richest group should prefer averaging from the top down. The rich would wish to be averaged with the second richest group before the latter had been reduced by averaging. The poor would prefer to be averaged with the second poorest group after the latter had been increased by averaging.

81. There are five columns of cities. Since cities in odd-numbered columns connect only with cities in even-numbered columns and vice versa, a tour must alternate between cities of each type. But there are ten cities in even-numbered columns and twelve in odd. Hence a continuous tour is impossible.

82. The second player should always win. Whenever his opponent plays card n, he should counter with the card valued 15 − n. He is bound to hit 60 on his fourth play.

83. Mother. If she says no the 1st night, she'll say yes the 2nd. If she says yes, Father is asked the 2nd night. In either case, permission for 2 consecutive nights out rests with him. By symmetry, success would depend on Mother if Father were asked first. Since Father is more permissive, Mother should be asked first.

84. He must pick up 7 shirts to tide him over until the following Monday. Hence he must deposit 7 shirts each Monday. Counting the shirt he wears on Monday, the required total is 15. (Note that he cannot get by with only 14 by exchanging his Monday shirt for a clean one and turning it in to the laundry, as he will be caught short the following Monday.)

85. Suppose otherwise and assume that there are n Irishmen. The possible number of Irish friends for a given Irishman ranges from 0 to n − 1, and each of these possibilities must be realized in order that all n numbers be different. However, if one Irishman is a friend of all the others, no Irishman can be friendless. Thus the 0 and the n − 1 are mutually inconsistent.

86. Yes, by considering the throws in pairs and deleting each occurrence of HH or TT. Since HT and TH are equiprobable, one may be used to denote 0, the other, 1.

87. Jones threw his first ball in the gutter in each of the first 9 frames (or in all but one of the first 9 frames in which he knocked down the first pin with his first ball) but managed to get spares on all of them. He ended with 3 consecutive strikes. Smith got 5 consecutive strikes followed by a three or a four. Thus Smith won 132 to 130, 131 to 130, or 132 to 131.

88. If A marries B's sister, B marries C's sister, and C marries A's sister, a group of three is possible. An additional mutual brother-in-law, however, is not possible without violating either the laws of bigamy or consanguinity.

89. Each lap after the first contributes one degree of uncertainty to the salesman's location. If there are N cities, N − 2 laps of N − 1, plus the first lap of N, plus one more city of the (N − 1)st lap will be necessary in order to make the salesman's whereabouts completely indeterminate. This gives a total of $N^2 - 2N + 3$ days or 83 days when N = 10. (On the 82nd day it could be definitely stated that he was not in the first city.)

90. The simplest method of determining who is a Dissembler, Soothsayer, or Diplomat is to ask the same question twice, "Are you a Diplomat?" Two "No's" would be a Soothsayer, two "Yes's" would uncover a Dissembler and a "No" and a "Yes" would mean that you are talking to a Diplomat.

91. Dan is oldest, shortest, and, next to Carl, the lightest.

92. 2, 1, and 3. The sequence represents the number of chimes of a wall clock which strikes once on the half hour, starting at noon or midnight.

93. The probability of a loaded face turning up is 1/5, of a given unloaded face 4/25. The probability of the two loaded faces turning up together is 1/25, of two unloaded faces adding to 7, 16/625. Since there are 5 such combinations, the total chance of throwing 7 is $1/25 + 5(16)/625 = 21/125$. Hence the effect of the loading is to increase the probability by $21/125 - 1/6$ or only one part in 750.

94. Prob. (L wrong, F right) = 1/3 · 3/4 = 1/4.
Prob. (F wrong, L right) = 1/4 · 2/3 = 1/6.
Hence the odds in favor of rain are 1/4 to 1/6 or 3 to 2, and prob. (rain) = 3/5.

95. The player's expectation, E, is $\frac{1}{2} + 4(\frac{1}{4}) + 9(\frac{1}{8}) + \ldots$, so that, by subtraction, $\frac{1}{2}E = \frac{1}{2} + 3(\frac{1}{4}) + 5(\frac{1}{8}) + \ldots$, and, subtracting again, $\frac{1}{4}E = \frac{1}{2} + 2(\frac{1}{4}) + 2(\frac{1}{8}) + \ldots$, so that $\frac{1}{4}E = \frac{1}{2} + 1$, or E = 6. Therefore the operator can expect to clear four dollars per game on the average.

96. The Series will end in 4, 5, 6, or 7 games with probs. ⅛, ¼, 5/16 and 5/16 respectively. The 6th and 7th games are played, if necessary, at the same park as the 1st and 2nd games. The desired probability is, therefore, ⅝.

97. The average number of empty cells when n balls are thrown into C cells is $\dfrac{(C-1)^n}{C^n-1}$.
If n = 5, C = 4, this becomes 243/256, so that the player's expectation is approximately 95¢. Hence the operator can expect to make a profit of a nickel a game on the average.

98. Not 3.5, since this is a case of sampling with replacement. Instead of summing $\sum_{n=1}^{\infty} \frac{n}{7}\left(\frac{6}{7}\right)^{n-1}$, use this shortcut. Each person has a $\frac{1}{7}$ probability of having been born on a Wednesday. In a sense then, each person is "1/7 of an expected Wednesday child." Since it requires 7 such to add up to a Wednesday child, the answer is 7 people.

99. With four specimens, the odds in favor of a mated triple are only 4/9. But if payload limitations permit five to travel to Earth, the odds go up to 50/81.

100. In the long run, the three black balls will occur equally spaced in the stream of balls which emerge. The player, therefore, can expect three white balls to appear before the first black ball and hence will show an average loss of a quarter a game.

101. Each of the 64 row and column pairs contain 15 numbered squares with one and only one number (the middle-ranking one) a candidate for saddle square. The number of permutations which retain the candidate at the row column intersection is $(7!)^2$ from a total of 15! possible arrangements. Since more than one saddle square is impossible, the required probability is $\dfrac{64(7!)^2}{15!} = .00124$.

102. If Max throws doubles, his chance of winning is $(5/6)^2$. If his two dice come up different, his chance is $(4/6)^2$. Thus his total probability is $1/6(5/6)^2 + 5/6(4/6)^2 = 105/216 \cong .486$. Bermuda, with a probability of .514, is the betting favorite.

103. If Vol. 4 is just right of Vol. 1, he eats through no pages at all; there are six such cases if we imagine the books arranged in all possible orders. Likewise he eats through 1, 2, 3, or 4 books if the volumes are arranged in any of 4, 8, 4, or 2 ways, respectively. (He will eat through 4 books, e.g., if they are arranged 4 2 3 1 or 4 3 2 1.) Therefore,
$$E_P = 300 \times \frac{6(0) + 4(1) + 8(2) + 4(3) + 2(4)}{24} = 500.$$

104. Either way, his estimate will be correct with the same probability, namely the proportion of the more abundant type of olive.

105. Normally his chance of firing the fatal bullet is 1/6. With each man spinning the chamber, the probability that the first five men survive is $(5/6)^5$, and his chance of being shot is 1/6 of that or about .067. Hence his survival probability is enhanced about .1 by spinning.

106. Let n be the number of coins in the bank. Then $15n + 10 = 14 (n + 1)$ and $n = 4$. Thus there are four coins totaling 60 cents, the only possibility being two nickels and two quarters.

107. The result is independent of order. With 3 wins and 2 losses, his final holdings are $32 (3/2)^3 (1/2)^2$ or 27 chips. Thus there was no profit, but a loss of 5 chips.

108. Of the $\binom{48}{2}$ different pairs of cards he could draw, there are $\binom{11}{2}$ diamond pairs and 16 pairs each of type 2-3, 2-4, 3-4, 3-7, 4-7, 4-8, 7-8, 7-9, or 8-9 which yield straights. One of each of the latter consists of 2 diamonds, i.e., has already been counted. The probability of a pat hand is therefore, $\dfrac{\binom{11}{2} + (15)(9)}{\binom{48}{2}}$ or about .168.

109. The partitions of 8 into 3 numbers are (6,1,1), (5,2,1), (4,3,1), (4,2,2), (3,3,2). Each partition involves either a duplication or 2 numbers with a sum of 7, neither of which can occur among 3 faces meeting at a corner of a correctly spotted die. Consequently, the probability of making 16 the hard way is zero.

110. Obviously the probabilities are the same since you and your partner are void in the same suit when and only when your opponents have all 13 cards in that suit and vice versa.

111. Assume two white marbles have been drawn. From the conditions given, the chance that the third marble is white is 1/2, i.e., there are an equal number of marbles of each color at this point. Hence w = b + 2 also $\dfrac{\binom{w}{2}}{\binom{w+b}{2}} = \dfrac{\binom{w}{2}}{\binom{2w-2}{2}} = 1/3$, so that $\dfrac{w(w-1)}{(2w-2)(2w-3)} = 1/3$, giving w = 6; b = 4.

112. If the probability that a team will win any particular game is p, the chance of winning the Series is $p^4 + 4p^4(1-p) + 10p^4(1-p)^2 + 20p^4(1-p)^3$. If this expression is equal to .4, p will be equal to .4539 approximately. Hence B's chance of winning the first game is .5461. Since odds of 6 to 5 correspond to a probability of only .5455 approximately, the gambler is on the safe side.

113. Let h be the probability of getting heads in a single throw. Then $h^2 = 1 - h$ and h is approximately 0.618.

114. Of $\binom{9}{3}$ possibilities, only the 3 rows, 3 columns, and 2 diagonals constitute a win. The answer is therefore, 2/21.

115. On a given match, the probability that all three coins come up the same is $(1/3)^2 = 1/9$, while the probability that all are different is, $2/3 \cdot 1/3 = 2/9$. Hence the probability that a given match results in a decision is 2/3, and the expected number of repetitions required to determine a loser is $\displaystyle\sum_{k=1}^{\infty} \frac{2}{3} k \left(\frac{1}{3}\right)^{k-1} = 1\frac{1}{2}$.

116. The 100 hundredth roots of unity are spaced uniformly about the unit circle. The "northernmost" root is i. Thus all the items mentioned are purely imaginary.

117. Perfection lies in 6 and 28.
13 should ne'er be seated at a feast.
And *Revelations* clearly indicate
The nature and true mark of the Beast. (See Rev. 13:18.)

118. $\dfrac{(3!)\,!}{(3!)\,(3!)}$ or $\binom{3+3}{3}$.

119. None of them is eccentric at all. Since an ecliptic is the apparent circular path of the sun during the planetary year, the eccentricity is zero.

120. Imagine 2 lead balls of equal mass, connected by a thin, loose filament, in the process of falling. If Aristotle were right, we would be faced with the absurd conclusion that severing the filament would delay impact!

121. . . . RB. can only be NEARBY and . . . LR . . . must be WALRUS. Then we can convert KVJZDC into ASYLU., which is obviously ASYLUM. FWF JID EQO WO?

122. Neither can reproduce. (The mule is a sterile hybrid, the product of a horse and a donkey or ass.)

123. Rearranging, we get $(x-y)^2 + (x-z)^2 + x^2 = 0$. Hence x = y = z = 0.

124. TEMBLOR and WIPEOUT.

125. A quick check of a calendar reveals that on leap years Jan., Feb., Mar., May, June, Sept., Oct., start on different days of the week. Likewise on non-leap years for Jan., Feb., Apr., May, June, Aug., and Sept. It follows that every year has at least one Friday the 13th.

126. All are prime. (See Wilson's Theorem and its converse.)

127. Let x be a term far out in the sequence. The next two terms are approximately rx and r^2x. By the defining equation, $r^2x = 3x + 2rx$ or $r^2 - 2r - 3 = 0$. Rejecting the negative root, $r = 3$.

128. There are $\binom{18}{6}$ ways of selecting the 6 holes. However, if 4 of the holes form the arms of a Greek Cross, the center square will also drop out. There are $4\binom{13}{2}$ such possibilities. Likewise there are 3 sets of 6 which result in 2 center squares falling out. Eliminating these cases, the solution is $18,564 - 312 - 3$ or 18,249, including reflections.

129. 99. This number holds true regardless of the manner in which the puzzle is assembled. The proof is trivial. We start with 100 pieces and end up with a single cluster. Each move reduces the total number of clusters by one. Hence 99 moves.

130. The misspelling of "errors" and "receive" are, of course, the first two errors. The third error is simply that there are only two errors in all.

131. Not at all. Every closed boundary must contain at least one pair of perpendicular segments forming an L. The 2nd player, therefore, can avoid defeat by completing each of his opponent's potential L's, drawing the foot whenever the 1st player makes a vertical connection and the upright whenever he makes a horizontal one.

132. Between Volumes 10 and 3. Evidently the librarian is shelving according to the *alphabetical* order of the volume numbers.

133. Each of these numbers (as also with "vier" in German or "три" in Russian) is equal to the number of letters in its name. Moreover, they are the *only* numbers in their respective languages with this property.

134. 20 is in A, 21 is in B. Set A contains numbers with an even (B with an odd) number of letters in their literal representation.

135. Backwards motion.

136. Inspection of the 2 code clues reveals that each letter of the word involved is also a letter of the literal form of the corresponding code digit, e.g., the first letter of EXTROVERT appears in the word SEVEN, which is the first digit of the code equivalent. "Reading through" the numbers 895173246, the only possible words are INVESTORS or INVENTORS.

137. Penguins are confined to the Southern hemisphere, peahens take care of the egg-laying, Hungary is land-locked, the University of Chicago has no football team, 19-point cribbage hands are impossible, as are solutions to the equation $e^{e^x} = 1$, since this implies $e^x = 0$, which holds for no value of x, real or complex. Thus each class is empty.

138. Approximately 240,000 miles, the earth-moon distance, since the earth is a "synchronous satellite" of the moon.

139. 198 days. Every day it increased its height by one half of its original height. In 198 days, it reproduced its height 99 times and was therefore 100 times its original height.

140.

3	7	7
2	2	5
4	9	6

← *Not Fibonacci*

141. Since $417 = 3(5!) + 2(4!) + 1(3!) + 3$, the first digit has progressed from 1 to 4, the 2nd from 1 to 3 and the 3rd from 1 to 2. The last 3 digits constitute the 3rd largest permutation of 1, 5, and 6. The 417th term is 432516.

142. Suppose the ratio is 2: Then A . . . B = 2 (B . . . A). Then $B + 10 = 2A$ and $A = 2B$ or $2B + 1$, implying $3B = 10$ in the first case and $3B = 8$ in the second. Neither provides an integral value of B. The ratios, 3, 5, 6, 7, and 8 are similarly disposed of.

143. He did. Since $499 > \sqrt{49,999}$ it follows that 49,999 has no non-trivial prime factors > 499 (since it has none smaller). Also, 499 is obviously not a factor of 49,999. Hence 49,999 is prime, and the factorization is complete.

144. Call it M. Obviously all N's from 2 to 10 divide M + 1 evenly. The smallest M with this property is $(5 \cdot 7 \cdot 8 \cdot 9) - 1$ or 2519.

145. Except for (3,5), all prime pairs are of the form (6N − 1, 6N + 1) with product $36N^2 - 1$. The digital sum being simply the residue modulo 9, we note that $36N^2 - 1 \equiv -1 \equiv 8 \pmod{9}$.

146. Let N = number of couples. If men and women alternate there are (N + 1)! cyclic arrangements for each sex and, therefore, N(N − 1)!(N − 1)! = N!(N − 1)! ways of combining them. Hence (2N − 1)! = 10N!(N − 1)! N = 3 is a solution while for N > 3 it is easily shown that the left member exceeds the right. Thus there are 3 couples who can sit in 5! or 120 ways as opposed to 12 ways if sexes alternate.

147. The longest possible chain will result when the ratio between successive numbers is as close as possible to $(1 + \sqrt{5})/2$. Therefore the penultimate value must be 618,034, and, working backward, the chain begins: 154, 144, 298, 442, ... 1,000,000 is the 20th link in the chain.

148. Let $A = \sqrt{2}^{\sqrt{2}}$. If A is rational, it is the desired example. On the other hand, if A is irrational, then $A^{\sqrt{2}} = 2$ is the desired example.

149. $999,919 = 1,000,000 - 81 = (1,000)^2 - 9^2 = (991)\ (1,009)$. $1,000,343 = (100^3 + 7^3)$. Since $x^3 + y^3$ factors into $(x + y)\ (x^2 - xy + y^2)$, 107 is a factor of 1,000,343.

150. There are 4 choices of wife for the oldest of the 6 boys. If his brother marries his wife's sister, 4 distinct pairings of the other people are possible. If not, 16 pairings are possible. The total is then 4(4 + 16) = 80.

151. For each octopus, there are $\binom{8}{4}$ choices for the tentacles pinned and 4! permutations of these 4 tentacles with respect to the opponent's pinning tentacles. The answer is, therefore, $\binom{8}{4}^2 (4!)^2 = 2,822,400$.

152. The number k is seen to occur first at the $\left(\dfrac{k(k - 1)}{2} + 1 \right)$th position. Calling this latter expression n and solving for k, $k = (1 + \sqrt{8n - 7})/2$. In general, by the nature of the progression, the nth term is the greatest integer $\leq$ this expression. The millionth term is, therefore, 1,414.

153. If P > 3, then P is of the form $6k \pm 1$ and $P^2 + 2 = 36k^2 \pm 12k + 3$, a multiple of 3. Hence for P and $P^2 + 2$ to be prime, P must be 3, in which case $P^2 + 4 = 13$ is indeed prime. (Thus, regretfully, the problem adds no support to the famous Twin Prime Conjecture.)

154. Any counting interval from 1 through 9 will result in another team member's selection. Joe will be captain if he chooses 10.

155. In any base, 2 = 40/20 < 41/14 < 44/11 = 4. Hence 41/14 = 3.
If B is the base, 4 B + 1 = 3 (B + 4), and B = 11. (The Puevigians use 11 as their base, since they have 5 fingers on one hand and 6 on the other.)

156. There are altogether 7^3 or 343 possibilities. Of these, 49 read the same backward or forward. Half the remaining 294 must be eliminated since they are duplicates. There are, therefore, a total of 196 pieces in the set.

157. The extreme digits can only be 2 and 8 or 1 and 9 with respective multipliers 4 and 9. In both cases there is no carry to the first (leftmost) digit, and the second digit of the smaller number is quickly found. It is 0 or 1 in the first case and 0 in the second. Now working at the other end, one arrives at 4 × 21978 = 87912 as the only solution satisfying the distinct digits condition.

158. A final zero can result only from the product of a 2 and a 5. Since there will be more 2's than 5's in N!, the number of final zeros will be the highest power of 5 in N!, which is 10 for 49! and 12 for 50!. Since 25!, 30!, 35!, and 40! have, respectively, 6, 7, 8, and 9 as the highest contained power of 5, the required number is 11.

A CATALOGUE OF
SELECTED DOVER BOOKS
IN ALL FIELDS OF INTEREST

A CATALOGUE OF SELECTED DOVER
BOOKS IN ALL FIELDS OF INTEREST

RACKHAM'S COLOR ILLUSTRATIONS FOR WAGNER'S RING. Rackham's finest mature work—all 64 full-color watercolors in a faithful and lush interpretation of the *Ring*. Full-sized plates on coated stock of the paintings used by opera companies for authentic staging of Wagner. Captions aid in following complete Ring cycle. Introduction. 64 illustrations plus vignettes. 72pp. 8⅝ x 11¼.   23779-6 Pa. $6.00

CONTEMPORARY POLISH POSTERS IN FULL COLOR, edited by Joseph Czestochowski. 46 full-color examples of brilliant school of Polish graphic design, selected from world's first museum (near Warsaw) dedicated to poster art. Posters on circuses, films, plays, concerts all show cosmopolitan influences, free imagination. Introduction. 48pp. 9⅜ x 12¼.
23780-X Pa. $6.00

GRAPHIC WORKS OF EDVARD MUNCH, Edvard Munch. 90 haunting, evocative prints by first major Expressionist artist and one of the greatest graphic artists of his time: *The Scream, Anxiety, Death Chamber, The Kiss, Madonna,* etc. Introduction by Alfred Werner. 90pp. 9 x 12.
23765-6 Pa. $5.00

THE GOLDEN AGE OF THE POSTER, Hayward and Blanche Cirker. 70 extraordinary posters in full colors, from Maitres de l'Affiche, Mucha, Lautrec, Bradley, Cheret, Beardsley, many others. Total of 78pp. 9⅜ x 12¼.   22753-7 Pa. $5.95

THE NOTEBOOKS OF LEONARDO DA VINCI, edited by J. P. Richter. Extracts from manuscripts reveal great genius; on painting, sculpture, anatomy, sciences, geography, etc. Both Italian and English. 186 ms. pages reproduced, plus 500 additional drawings, including studies for *Last Supper,* Sforza monument, etc. 860pp. 7⅞ x 10¾. (Available in U.S. only)
22572-0, 22573-9 Pa., Two-vol. set $15.90

THE CODEX NUTTALL, as first edited by Zelia Nuttall. Only inexpensive edition, in full color, of a pre-Columbian Mexican (Mixtec) book. 88 color plates show kings, gods, heroes, temples, sacrifices. New explanatory, historical introduction by Arthur G. Miller. 96pp. 11⅜ x 8½. (Available in U.S. only)   23168-2 Pa. $7.95

UNE SEMAINE DE BONTÉ, A SURREALISTIC NOVEL IN COLLAGE, Max Ernst. Masterpiece created out of 19th-century periodical illustrations, explores worlds of terror and surprise. Some consider this Ernst's greatest work. 208pp. 8⅛ x 11.   23252-2 Pa. $6.00

DRAWINGS OF WILLIAM BLAKE, William Blake. 92 plates from Book of Job, *Divine Comedy, Paradise Lost,* visionary heads, mythological figures, Laocoon, etc. Selection, introduction, commentary by Sir Geoffrey Keynes. 178pp. 8⅛ x 11. 22303-5 Pa. $4.00

ENGRAVINGS OF HOGARTH, William Hogarth. 101 of Hogarth's greatest works: *Rake's Progress, Harlot's Progress, Illustrations for Hudibras, Before and After, Beer Street and Gin Lane,* many more. Full commentary. 256pp. 11 x 13¾. 22479-1 Pa. $12.95

DAUMIER: 120 GREAT LITHOGRAPHS, Honore Daumier. Wide-ranging collection of lithographs by the greatest caricaturist of the 19th century. Concentrates on eternally popular series on lawyers, on married life, on liberated women, etc. Selection, introduction, and notes on plates by Charles F. Ramus. Total of 158pp. 9⅜ x 12¼. 23512-2 Pa. $6.00

DRAWINGS OF MUCHA, Alphonse Maria Mucha. Work reveals drafts-man of highest caliber: studies for famous posters and paintings, render-ings for book illustrations and ads, etc. 70 works, 9 in color; including 6 items not drawings. Introduction. List of illustrations. 72pp. 9⅜ x 12¼. (Available in U.S. only) 23672-2 Pa. $4.00

GIOVANNI BATTISTA PIRANESI: DRAWINGS IN THE PIERPONT MORGAN LIBRARY, Giovanni Battista Piranesi. For first time ever all of Morgan Library's collection, world's largest. 167 illustrations of rare Piranesi drawings—archeological, architectural, decorative and visionary. Essay, detailed list of drawings, chronology, captions. Edited by Felice Stampfle. 144pp. 9⅜ x 12¼. 23714-1 Pa. $7.50

NEW YORK ETCHINGS (1905-1949), John Sloan. All of important American artist's N.Y. life etchings. 67 works include some of his best art; also lively historical record—Greenwich Village, tenement scenes. Edited by Sloan's widow. Introduction and captions. 79pp. 8⅜ x 11¼. 23651-X Pa. $4.00

CHINESE PAINTING AND CALLIGRAPHY: A PICTORIAL SURVEY, Wan-go Weng. 69 fine examples from John M. Crawford's matchless private collection: landscapes, birds, flowers, human figures, etc., plus calligraphy. Every basic form included: hanging scrolls, handscrolls, album leaves, fans, etc. 109 illustrations. Introduction. Captions. 192pp. 8⅞ x 11¾. 23707-9 Pa. $7.95

DRAWINGS OF REMBRANDT, edited by Seymour Slive. Updated Lipp-mann, Hofstede de Groot edition, with definitive scholarly apparatus. All portraits, biblical sketches, landscapes, nudes, Oriental figures, classical studies, together with selection of work by followers. 550 illustrations. Total of 630pp. 9⅛ x 12¼. 21485-0, 21486-9 Pa., Two-vol. set $15.00

THE DISASTERS OF WAR, Francisco Goya. 83 etchings record horrors of Napoleonic wars in Spain and war in general. Reprint of 1st edition, plus 3 additional plates. Introduction by Philip Hofer. 97pp. 9⅜ x 8¼. 21872-4 Pa. $4.00

THE EARLY WORK OF AUBREY BEARDSLEY, Aubrey Beardsley. 157 plates, 2 in color: *Manon Lescaut, Madame Bovary, Morte Darthur, Salome,* other. Introduction by H. Marillier. 182pp. 8⅛ x 11. 21816-3 Pa. $4.50

THE LATER WORK OF AUBREY BEARDSLEY, Aubrey Beardsley. Exotic masterpieces of full maturity: *Venus and Tannhauser, Lysistrata, Rape of the Lock, Volpone,* Savoy material, etc. 174 plates, 2 in color. 186pp. 8⅛ x 11. 21817-1 Pa. $5.95

THOMAS NAST'S CHRISTMAS DRAWINGS, Thomas Nast. Almost all Christmas drawings by creator of image of Santa Claus as we know it, and one of America's foremost illustrators and political cartoonists. 66 illustrations. 3 illustrations in color on covers. 96pp. 8⅜ x 11¼. 23660-9 Pa. $3.50

THE DORÉ ILLUSTRATIONS FOR DANTE'S DIVINE COMEDY, Gustave Doré. All 135 plates from Inferno, Purgatory, Paradise; fantastic tortures, infernal landscapes, celestial wonders. Each plate with appropriate (translated) verses. 141pp. 9 x 12. 23231-X Pa. $4.50

DORÉ'S ILLUSTRATIONS FOR RABELAIS, Gustave Doré. 252 striking illustrations of *Gargantua and Pantagruel* books by foremost 19th-century illustrator. Including 60 plates, 192 delightful smaller illustrations. 153pp. 9 x 12. 23656-0 Pa. $5.00

LONDON: A PILGRIMAGE, Gustave Doré, Blanchard Jerrold. Squalor, riches, misery, beauty of mid-Victorian metropolis; 55 wonderful plates, 125 other illustrations, full social, cultural text by Jerrold. 191pp. of text. 9⅜ x 12¼. 22306-X Pa. $7.00

THE RIME OF THE ANCIENT MARINER, Gustave Doré, S. T. Coleridge. Dore's finest work, 34 plates capture moods, subtleties of poem. Full text. Introduction by Millicent Rose. 77pp. 9¼ x 12. 22305-1 Pa. $3.50

THE DORE BIBLE ILLUSTRATIONS, Gustave Doré. All wonderful, detailed plates: Adam and Eve, Flood, Babylon, Life of Jesus, etc. Brief King James text with each plate. Introduction by Millicent Rose. 241 plates. 241pp. 9 x 12. 23004-X Pa. $6.00

THE COMPLETE ENGRAVINGS, ETCHINGS AND DRYPOINTS OF ALBRECHT DURER. "Knight, Death and Devil"; "Melencolia," and more—all Dürer's known works in all three media, including 6 works formerly attributed to him. 120 plates. 235pp. 8⅜ x 11¼. 22851-7 Pa. $6.50

MECHANICK EXERCISES ON THE WHOLE ART OF PRINTING, Joseph Moxon. First complete book (1683-4) ever written about typography, a compendium of everything known about printing at the latter part of 17th century. Reprint of 2nd (1962) Oxford Univ. Press edition. 74 illustrations. Total of 550pp. 6⅛ x 9¼. 23617-X Pa. $7.95

THE COMPLETE WOODCUTS OF ALBRECHT DURER, edited by Dr. W. Kurth. 346 in all: "Old Testament," "St. Jerome," "Passion," "Life of Virgin," Apocalypse," many others. Introduction by Campbell Dodgson. 285pp. 8½ x 12¼.   21097-9 Pa. $7.50

DRAWINGS OF ALBRECHT DURER, edited by Heinrich Wolfflin. 81 plates show development from youth to full style. Many favorites; many new. Introduction by Alfred Werner. 96pp. 8⅛ x 11.   22352-3 Pa. $5.00

THE HUMAN FIGURE, Albrecht Dürer. Experiments in various techniques—stereometric, progressive proportional, and others. Also life studies that rank among finest ever done. Complete reprinting of *Dresden Sketchbook*. 170 plates. 355pp. 8⅜ x 11¼.   21042-1 Pa. $7.95

OF THE JUST SHAPING OF LETTERS, Albrecht Dürer. Renaissance artist explains design of Roman majuscules by geometry, also Gothic lower and capitals. Grolier Club edition. 43pp. 7⅞ x 10¾   21306-4 Pa. $3.00

TEN BOOKS ON ARCHITECTURE, Vitruvius. The most important book ever written on architecture. Early Roman aesthetics, technology, classical orders, site selection, all other aspects. Stands behind everything since. Morgan translation. 331pp. 5⅜ x 8½.   20645-9 Pa. $4.50

THE FOUR BOOKS OF ARCHITECTURE, Andrea Palladio. 16th-century classic responsible for Palladian movement and style. Covers classical architectural remains, Renaissance revivals, classical orders, etc. 1738 Ware English edition. Introduction by A. Placzek. 216 plates. 110pp. of text. 9½ x 12¾.   21308-0 Pa. $10.00

HORIZONS, Norman Bel Geddes. Great industrialist stage designer, "father of streamlining," on application of aesthetics to transportation, amusement, architecture, etc. 1932 prophetic account; function, theory, specific projects. 222 illustrations. 312pp. 7⅞ x 10¾.   23514-9 Pa. $6.95

FRANK LLOYD WRIGHT'S FALLINGWATER, Donald Hoffmann. Full, illustrated story of conception and building of Wright's masterwork at Bear Run, Pa. 100 photographs of site, construction, and details of completed structure. 112pp. 9¼ x 10.   23671-4 Pa. $5.50

THE ELEMENTS OF DRAWING, John Ruskin. Timeless classic by great Viltorian; starts with basic ideas, works through more difficult. Many practical exercises. 48 illustrations. Introduction by Lawrence Campbell. 228pp. 5⅜ x 8½.   22730-8 Pa. $3.75

GIST OF ART, John Sloan. Greatest modern American teacher, Art Students League, offers innumerable hints, instructions, guided comments to help you in painting. Not a formal course. 46 illustrations. Introduction by Helen Sloan. 200pp. 5⅜ x 8½.   23435-5 Pa. $4.00

THE ANATOMY OF THE HORSE, George Stubbs. Often considered the great masterpiece of animal anatomy. Full reproduction of 1766 edition, plus prospectus; original text and modernized text. 36 plates. Introduction by Eleanor Garvey. 121pp. 11 x 14¾. 23402-9 Pa. $6.00

BRIDGMAN'S LIFE DRAWING, George B. Bridgman. More than 500 illustrative drawings and text teach you to abstract the body into its major masses, use light and shade, proportion; as well as specific areas of anatomy, of which Bridgman is master. 192pp. 6½ x 9¼. (Available in U.S. only) 22710-3 Pa. $3.50

ART NOUVEAU DESIGNS IN COLOR, Alphonse Mucha, Maurice Verneuil, Georges Auriol. Full-color reproduction of *Combinaisons ornementales* (c. 1900) by Art Nouveau masters. Floral, animal, geometric, interlacings, swashes—borders, frames, spots—all incredibly beautiful. 60 plates, hundreds of designs. 9⅜ x 8-1/16. 22885-1 Pa. $4.00

FULL-COLOR FLORAL DESIGNS IN THE ART NOUVEAU STYLE, E. A. Seguy. 166 motifs, on 40 plates, from *Les fleurs et leurs applications decoratives* (1902): borders, circular designs, repeats, allovers, "spots." All in authentic Art Nouveau colors. 48pp. 9⅜ x 12¼. 23439-8 Pa. $5.00

A DIDEROT PICTORIAL ENCYCLOPEDIA OF TRADES AND INDUSTRY, edited by Charles C. Gillispie. 485 most interesting plates from the great French Encyclopedia of the 18th century show hundreds of working figures, artifacts, process, land and cityscapes; glassmaking, papermaking, metal extraction, construction, weaving, making furniture, clothing, wigs, dozens of other activities. Plates fully explained. 920pp. 9 x 12. 22284-5, 22285-3 Clothbd., Two-vol. set $40.00

HANDBOOK OF EARLY ADVERTISING ART, Clarence P. Hornung. Largest collection of copyright-free early and antique advertising art ever compiled. Over 6,000 illustrations, from Franklin's time to the 1890's for special effects, novelty. Valuable source, almost inexhaustible.
Pictorial Volume. Agriculture, the zodiac, animals, autos, birds, Christmas, fire engines, flowers, trees, musical instruments, ships, games and sports, much more. Arranged by subject matter and use. 237 plates. 288pp. 9 x 12. 20122-8 Clothbd. $14.50

Typographical Volume. Roman and Gothic faces ranging from 10 point to 300 point, "Barnum," German and Old English faces, script, logotypes, scrolls and flourishes, 1115 ornamental initials, 67 complete alphabets, more. 310 plates. 320pp. 9 x 12. 20123-6 Clothbd. $15.00

CALLIGRAPHY (CALLIGRAPHIA LATINA), J. G. Schwandner. High point of 18th-century ornamental calligraphy. Very ornate initials, scrolls, borders, cherubs, birds, lettered examples. 172pp. 9 x 13. 20475-8 Pa. $7.00

ART FORMS IN NATURE, Ernst Haeckel. Multitude of strangely beautiful natural forms: Radiolaria, Foraminifera, jellyfishes, fungi, turtles, bats, etc. All 100 plates of the 19th-century evolutionist's *Kunstformen der Natur* (1904). 100pp. 9⅜ x 12¼. 22987-4 Pa. $5.00

CHILDREN: A PICTORIAL ARCHIVE FROM NINETEENTH-CENTURY SOURCES, edited by Carol Belanger Grafton. 242 rare, copyright-free wood engravings for artists and designers. Widest such selection available. All illustrations in line. 119pp. 8⅜ x 11¼. 23694-3 Pa. $4.00

WOMEN: A PICTORIAL ARCHIVE FROM NINETEENTH-CENTURY SOURCES, edited by Jim Harter. 391 copyright-free wood engravings for artists and designers selected from rare periodicals. Most extensive such collection available. All illustrations in line. 128pp. 9 x 12. 23703-6 Pa. $4.50

ARABIC ART IN COLOR, Prisse d'Avennes. From the greatest ornamentalists of all time—50 plates in color, rarely seen outside the Near East, rich in suggestion and stimulus. Includes 4 plates on covers. 46pp. 9⅜ x 12¼. 23658-7 Pa. $6.00

AUTHENTIC ALGERIAN CARPET DESIGNS AND MOTIFS, edited by June Beveridge. Algerian carpets are world famous. Dozens of geometrical motifs are charted on grids, color-coded, for weavers, needleworkers, craftsmen, designers. 53 illustrations plus 4 in color. 48pp. 8¼ x 11. (Available in U.S. only) 23650-1 Pa. $1.75

DICTIONARY OF AMERICAN PORTRAITS, edited by Hayward and Blanche Cirker. 4000 important Americans, earliest times to 1905, mostly in clear line. Politicians, writers, soldiers, scientists, inventors, industrialists, Indians, Blacks, women, outlaws, etc. Identificatory information. 756pp. 9¼ x 12¾. 21823-6 Clothbd. $40.00

HOW THE OTHER HALF LIVES, Jacob A. Riis. Journalistic record of filth, degradation, upward drive in New York immigrant slums, shops, around 1900. New edition includes 100 original Riis photos, monuments of early photography. 233pp. 10 x 7⅞. 22012-5 Pa. $7.00

NEW YORK IN THE THIRTIES, Berenice Abbott. Noted photographer's fascinating study of city shows new buildings that have become famous and old sights that have disappeared forever. Insightful commentary. 97 photographs. 97pp. 11⅜ x 10. 22967-X Pa. $5.00

MEN AT WORK, Lewis W. Hine. Famous photographic studies of construction workers, railroad men, factory workers and coal miners. New supplement of 18 photos on Empire State building construction. New introduction by Jonathan L. Doherty. Total of 69 photos. 63pp. 8 x 10¾. 23475-4 Pa. $3.00

THE DEPRESSION YEARS AS PHOTOGRAPHED BY ARTHUR ROTH-
STEIN, Arthur Rothstein. First collection devoted entirely to the work of
outstanding 1930s photographer: famous dust storm photo, ragged children,
unemployed, etc. 120 photographs. Captions. 119pp. 9¼ x 10¾.
23590-4 Pa. $5.00

CAMERA WORK: A PICTORIAL GUIDE, Alfred Stieglitz. All 559 illustrations and plates from the most important periodical in the history of
art photography, Camera Work (1903-17). Presented four to a page, reduced in size but still clear, in strict chronological order, with complete
captions. Three indexes. Glossary. Bibliography. 176pp. 8⅜ x 11¼.
23591-2 Pa. $6.95

ALVIN LANGDON COBURN, PHOTOGRAPHER, Alvin L. Coburn. Revealing autobiography by one of greatest photographers of 20th century
gives insider's version of Photo-Secession, plus comments on his own work.
77 photographs by Coburn. Edited by Helmut and Alison Gernsheim.
160pp. 8⅛ x 11.
23685-4 Pa. $6.00

NEW YORK IN THE FORTIES, Andreas Feininger. 162 brilliant photographs by the well-known photographer, formerly with Life magazine, show
commuters, shoppers, Times Square at night, Harlem nightclub, Lower
East Side, etc. Introduction and full captions by John von Hartz. 181pp.
9¼ x 10¾.
23585-8 Pa. $6.95

GREAT NEWS PHOTOS AND THE STORIES BEHIND THEM, John
Faber. Dramatic volume of 140 great news photos, 1855 through 1976,
and revealing stories behind them, with both historical and technical information. Hindenburg disaster, shooting of Oswald, nomination of Jimmy
Carter, etc. 160pp. 8¼ x 11.
23667-6 Pa. $5.00

THE ART OF THE CINEMATOGRAPHER, Leonard Maltin. Survey of
American cinematography history and anecdotal interviews with 5 masters—
Arthur Miller, Hal Mohr, Hal Rosson, Lucien Ballard, and Conrad Hall.
Very large selection of behind-the-scenes production photos. 105 photographs. Filmographies. Index. Originally Behind the Camera. 144pp.
8¼ x 11.
23686-2 Pa. $5.00

DESIGNS FOR THE THREE-CORNERED HAT (LE TRICORNE),
Pablo Picasso. 32 fabulously rare drawings—including 31 color illustrations
of costumes and accessories—for 1919 production of famous ballet. Edited
by Parmenia Migel, who has written new introduction. 48pp. 9⅜ x 12¼.
(Available in U.S. only)
23709-5 Pa. $5.00

NOTES OF A FILM DIRECTOR, Sergei Eisenstein. Greatest Russian
filmmaker explains montage, making of Alexander Nevsky, aesthetics; comments on self, associates, great rivals (Chaplin), similar material. 78 illustrations. 240pp. 5⅜ x 8½.
22392-2 Pa. $4.50

HOLLYWOOD GLAMOUR PORTRAITS, edited by John Kobal. 145 photos capture the stars from 1926-49, the high point in portrait photography. Gable, Harlow, Bogart, Bacall, Hedy Lamarr, Marlene Dietrich, Robert Montgomery, Marlon Brando, Veronica Lake; 94 stars in all. Full background on photographers, technical aspects, much more. Total of 160pp. 8⅜ x 11¼.   23352-9 Pa. $6.00

THE NEW YORK STAGE: FAMOUS·PRODUCTIONS IN PHOTO-GRAPHS, edited by Stanley Appelbaum. 148 photographs from Museum of City of New York show 142 plays, 1883-1939. *Peter Pan, The Front Page, Dead End, Our Town,* O'Neill, hundreds of actors and actresses, etc. Full indexes. 154pp. 9½ x 10.   23241-7 Pa. $6.00

DIALOGUES CONCERNING TWO NEW SCIENCES, Galileo Galilei. Encompassing 30 years of experiment and thought, these dialogues deal with geometric demonstrations of fracture of solid bodies, cohesion, leverage, speed of light and sound, pendulums, falling bodies, accelerated motion, etc. 300pp. 5⅜ x 8½.   60099-8 Pa. $4.00

THE GREAT OPERA STARS IN HISTORIC PHOTOGRAPHS, edited by James Camner. 343 portraits from the 1850s to the 1940s: Tamburini, Mario, Caliapin, Jeritza, Melchior, Melba, Patti, Pinza, Schipa, Caruso, Farrar, Steber, Gobbi, and many more—270 performers in all. Index. 199pp. 8⅜ x 11¼.   23575-0 Pa. $7.50

J. S. BACH, Albert Schweitzer. Great full-length study of Bach, life, background to music, music, by foremost modern scholar. Ernest Newman translation. 650 musical examples. Total of 928pp. 5⅜ x 8½. (Available in U.S. only)   21631-4, 21632-2 Pa., Two-vol. set $11.00

COMPLETE PIANO SONATAS, Ludwig van Beethoven. All sonatas in the fine Schenker edition, with fingering, analytical material. One of best modern editions. Total of 615pp. 9 x 12. (Available in U.S. only)
                                23134-8, 23135-6 Pa., Two-vol. set $15.50

KEYBOARD MUSIC, J. S. Bach. Bach-Gesellschaft edition. For harpsichord, piano, other keyboard instruments. English Suites, French Suites, Six Partitas, Goldberg Variations, Two-Part Inventions, Three-Part Sinfonias. 312pp. 8⅛ x 11. (Available in U.S. only)   22360-4 Pa. $6.95

FOUR SYMPHONIES IN FULL SCORE, Franz Schubert. Schubert's four most popular symphonies: No. 4 in C Minor ("Tragic"); No. 5 in B-flat Major; No. 8 in B Minor ("Unfinished"); No. 9 in C Major ("Great"). Breitkopf & Hartel edition. Study score. 261pp. 9⅜ x 12¼.
                                                           23681-1 Pa. $6.50

THE AUTHENTIC GILBERT & SULLIVAN SONGBOOK, W. S. Gilbert, A. S. Sullivan. Largest selection available; 92 songs, uncut, original keys, in piano rendering approved by Sullivan. Favorites and lesser-known fine numbers. Edited with plot synopses by James Spero. 3 illustrations. 399pp. 9 x 12.   23482-7 Pa. $9.95

PRINCIPLES OF ORCHESTRATION, Nikolay Rimsky-Korsakov. Great classical orchestrator provides fundamentals of tonal resonance, progression of parts, voice and orchestra, tutti effects, much else in major document. 330pp. of musical excerpts. 489pp. 6½ x 9¼.   21266-1 Pa. $7.50

TRISTAN UND ISOLDE, Richard Wagner. Full orchestral score with complete instrumentation. Do not confuse with piano reduction. Commentary by Felix Mottl, great Wagnerian conductor and scholar. Study score. 655pp. 8⅛ x 11.   22915-7 Pa. $13.95

REQUIEM IN FULL SCORE, Giuseppe Verdi. Immensely popular with choral groups and music lovers. Republication of edition published by C. F. Peters, Leipzig, n. d. German frontmaker in English translation. Glossary. Text in Latin. Study score. 204pp. 9⅜ x 12¼.
23682-X Pa. $6.00

COMPLETE CHAMBER MUSIC FOR STRINGS, Felix Mendelssohn. All of Mendelssohn's chamber music: Octet, 2 Quintets, 6 Quartets, and Four Pieces for String Quartet. (Nothing with piano is included). Complete works edition (1874-7). Study score. 283 pp. 9⅜ x 12¼.
23679-X Pa. $7.50

POPULAR SONGS OF NINETEENTH-CENTURY AMERICA, edited by Richard Jackson. 64 most important songs: "Old Oaken Bucket," "Arkansas Traveler," "Yellow Rose of Texas," etc. Authentic original sheet music, full introduction and commentaries. 290pp. 9 x 12.   23270-0 Pa. $7.95

COLLECTED PIANO WORKS, Scott Joplin. Edited by Vera Brodsky Lawrence. Practically all of Joplin's piano works—rags, two-steps, marches, waltzes, etc., 51 works in all. Extensive introduction by Rudi Blesh. Total of 345pp. 9 x 12.   23106-2 Pa. $14.95

BASIC PRINCIPLES OF CLASSICAL BALLET, Agrippina Vaganova. Great Russian theoretician, teacher explains methods for teaching classical ballet; incorporates best from French, Italian, Russian schools. 118 illustrations. 175pp. 5⅜ x 8½.   22036-2 Pa. $2.50

CHINESE CHARACTERS, L. Wieger. Rich analysis of 2300 characters according to traditional systems into primitives. Historical-semantic analysis to phonetics (Classical Mandarin) and radicals. 820pp. 6⅛ x 9¼.
21321-8 Pa. $10.00

EGYPTIAN LANGUAGE: EASY LESSONS IN EGYPTIAN HIERO-GLYPHICS, E. A. Wallis Budge. Foremost Egyptologist offers Egyptian grammar, explanation of hieroglyphics, many reading texts, dictionary of symbols. 246pp. 5 x 7½. (Available in U.S. only)
21394-3 Clothbd. $7.50

AN ETYMOLOGICAL DICTIONARY OF MODERN ENGLISH, Ernest Weekley. Richest, fullest work, by foremost British lexicographer. Detailed word histories. Inexhaustible. Do not confuse this with Concise Etymological Dictionary, which is abridged. Total of 856pp. 6½ x 9¼.
21873-2, 21874-0 Pa., Two-vol. set $12.00

A MAYA GRAMMAR, Alfred M. Tozzer. Practical, useful English-language grammar by the Harvard anthropologist who was one of the three greatest American scholars in the area of Maya culture. Phonetics, grammatical processes, syntax, more. 301pp. 5⅜ x 8½.   23465-7 Pa. $4.00

THE JOURNAL OF HENRY D. THOREAU, edited by Bradford Torrey, F. H. Allen. Complete reprinting of 14 volumes, 1837-61, over two million words; the sourcebooks for *Walden,* etc. Definitive. All original sketches, plus 75 photographs. Introduction by Walter Harding. Total of 1804pp. 8½ x 12¼.   20312-3, 20313-1 Clothbd., Two-vol. set $70.00

CLASSIC GHOST STORIES, Charles Dickens and others. 18 wonderful stories you've wanted to reread: "The Monkey's Paw," "The House and the Brain," "The Upper Berth," "The Signalman," "Dracula's Guest," "The Tapestried Chamber," etc. Dickens, Scott, Mary Shelley, Stoker, etc. 330pp. 5⅜ x 8½.   20735-8 Pa. $4.50

SEVEN SCIENCE FICTION NOVELS, H. G. Wells. Full novels. *First Men in the Moon, Island of Dr. Moreau, War of the Worlds, Food of the Gods, Invisible Man, Time Machine, In the Days of the Comet.* A basic science-fiction library. 1015pp. 5⅜ x 8½. (Available in U.S. only)
20264-X Clothbd. $8.95

ARMADALE, Wilkie Collins. Third great mystery novel by the author of *The Woman in White* and *The Moonstone.* Ingeniously plotted narrative shows an exceptional command of character, incident and mood. Original magazine version with 40 illustrations. 597pp. 5⅜ x 8½.
23429-0 Pa. $6.00

MASTERS OF MYSTERY, H. Douglas Thomson. The first book in English (1931) devoted to history and aesthetics of detective story. Poe, Doyle, LeFanu, Dickens, many others, up to 1930. New introduction and notes by E. F. Bleiler. 288pp. 5⅜ x 8½. (Available in U.S. only)
23606-4 Pa. $4.00

FLATLAND, E. A. Abbott. Science-fiction classic explores life of 2-D being in 3-D world. Read also as introduction to thought about hyperspace. Introduction by Banesh Hoffmann. 16 illustrations. 103pp. 5⅜ x 8½.
20001-9 Pa. $2.00

THREE SUPERNATURAL NOVELS OF THE VICTORIAN PERIOD, edited, with an introduction, by E. F. Bleiler. Reprinted complete and unabridged, three great classics of the supernatural: *The Haunted Hotel* by Wilkie Collins, *The Haunted House at Latchford* by Mrs. J. H. Riddell, and *The Lost Stradivarious* by J. Meade Falkner. 325pp. 5⅜ x 8½.
22571-2 Pa. $4.00

AYESHA: THE RETURN OF "SHE," H. Rider Haggard. Virtuoso sequel featuring the great mythic creation, Ayesha, in an adventure that is fully as good as the first book, *She.* Original magazine version, with 47 original illustrations by Maurice Greiffenhagen. 189pp. 6½ x 9¼.
23649-8 Pa. $3.50

UNCLE SILAS, J. Sheridan LeFanu. Victorian Gothic mystery novel, considered by many best of period, even better than Collins or Dickens. Wonderful psychological terror. Introduction by Frederick Shroyer. 436pp. 5⅜ x 8½. 21715-9 Pa. $6.00

JURGEN, James Branch Cabell. The great erotic fantasy of the 1920's that delighted thousands, shocked thousands more. Full final text, Lane edition with 13 plates by Frank Pape. 346pp. 5⅜ x 8½.
23507-6 Pa. $4.50

THE CLAVERINGS, Anthony Trollope. Major novel, chronicling aspects of British Victorian society, personalities. Reprint of Cornhill serialization, 16 plates by M. Edwards; first reprint of full text. Introduction by Norman Donaldson. 412pp. 5⅜ x 8½. 23464-9 Pa. $5.00

KEPT IN THE DARK, Anthony Trollope. Unusual short novel about Victorian morality and abnormal psychology by the great English author. Probably the first American publication. Frontispiece by Sir John Millais. 92pp. 6½ x 9¼. 23609-9 Pa. $2.50

RALPH THE HEIR, Anthony Trollope. Forgotten tale of illegitimacy, inheritance. Master novel of Trollope's later years. Victorian country estates, clubs, Parliament, fox hunting, world of fully realized characters. Reprint of 1871 edition. 12 illustrations by F. A. Faser. 434pp. of text. 5⅜ x 8½. 23642-0 Pa. $5.00

YEKL and THE IMPORTED BRIDEGROOM AND OTHER STORIES OF THE NEW YORK GHETTO, Abraham Cahan. Film *Hester Street* based on *Yekl* (1896). Novel, other stories among first about Jewish immigrants of N.Y.'s East Side. Highly praised by W. D. Howells—Cahan "a new star of realism." New introduction by Bernard G. Richards. 240pp. 5⅜ x 8½. 22427-9 Pa. $3.50

THE HIGH PLACE, James Branch Cabell. Great fantasy writer's enchanting comedy of disenchantment set in 18th-century France. Considered by some critics to be even better than his famous *Jurgen*. 10 illustrations and numerous vignettes by noted fantasy artist Frank C. Pape. 320pp. 5⅜ x 8½. 23670-6 Pa. $4.00

ALICE'S ADVENTURES UNDER GROUND, Lewis Carroll. Facsimile of ms. Carroll gave Alice Liddell in 1864. Different in many ways from final Alice. Handlettered, illustrated by Carroll. Introduction by Martin Gardner. 128pp. 5⅜ x 8½. 21482-6 Pa. $2.50

FAVORITE ANDREW LANG FAIRY TALE BOOKS IN MANY COLORS, Andrew Lang. The four Lang favorites in a boxed set—the complete *Red, Green, Yellow* and *Blue* Fairy Books. 164 stories; 439 illustrations by Lancelot Speed, Henry Ford and G. P. Jacomb Hood. Total of about 1500pp. 5⅜ x 8½. 23407-X Boxed set, Pa. $15.95

HOUSEHOLD STORIES BY THE BROTHERS GRIMM. All the great Grimm stories: "Rumpelstiltskin," "Snow White," "Hansel and Gretel," etc., with 114 illustrations by Walter Crane. 269pp. 5⅜ x 8½.
21080-4 Pa. $3.50

SLEEPING BEAUTY, illustrated by Arthur Rackham. Perhaps the fullest, most delightful version ever, told by C. S. Evans. Rackham's best work. 49 illustrations. 110pp. 7⅞ x 10¾. 22756-1 Pa. $2.50

AMERICAN FAIRY TALES, L. Frank Baum. Young cowboy lassoes Father Time; dummy in Mr. Floman's department store window comes to life; and 10 other fairy tales. 41 illustrations by N. P. Hall, Harry Kennedy, Ike Morgan, and Ralph Gardner. 209pp. 5⅜ x 8½. 23643-9 Pa. $3.00

THE WONDERFUL WIZARD OF OZ, L. Frank Baum. Facsimile in full color of America's finest children's classic. Introduction by Martin Gardner. 143 illustrations by W. W. Denslow. 267pp. 5⅜ x 8½.
20691-2 Pa. $3.50

THE TALE OF PETER RABBIT, Beatrix Potter. The inimitable Peter's terrifying adventure in Mr. McGregor's garden, with all 27 wonderful, full-color Potter illustrations. 55pp. 4¼ x 5½. (Available in U.S. only)
22827-4 Pa. $1.25

THE STORY OF KING ARTHUR AND HIS KNIGHTS, Howard Pyle. Finest children's version of life of King Arthur. 48 illustrations by Pyle. 131pp. 6⅛ x 9¼. 21445-1 Pa. $4.95

CARUSO'S CARICATURES, Enrico Caruso. Great tenor's remarkable caricatures of self, fellow musicians, composers, others. Toscanini, Puccini, Farrar, etc. Impish, cutting, insightful. 473 illustrations. Preface by M. Sisca. 217pp. 8⅜ x 11¼. 23528-9 Pa. $6.95

PERSONAL NARRATIVE OF A PILGRIMAGE TO ALMADINAH AND MECCAH, Richard Burton. Great travel classic by remarkably colorful personality. Burton, disguised as a Moroccan, visited sacred shrines of Islam, narrowly escaping death. Wonderful observations of Islamic life, customs, personalities. 47 illustrations. Total of 959pp. 5⅜ x 8½.
21217-3, 21218-1 Pa., Two-vol. set $12.00

INCIDENTS OF TRAVEL IN YUCATAN, John L. Stephens. Classic (1843) exploration of jungles of Yucatan, looking for evidences of Maya civilization. Travel adventures, Mexican and Indian culture, etc. Total of 669pp. 5⅜ x 8½. 20926-1, 20927-X Pa., Two-vol. set $7.90

AMERICAN LITERARY AUTOGRAPHS FROM WASHINGTON IRVING TO HENRY JAMES, Herbert Cahoon, et al. Letters, poems, manuscripts of Hawthorne, Thoreau, Twain, Alcott, Whitman, 67 other prominent American authors. Reproductions, full transcripts and commentary. Plus checklist of all American Literary Autographs in The Pierpont Morgan Library. Printed on exceptionally high-quality paper. 136 illustrations. 212pp. 9⅛ x 12¼. 23548-3 Pa. $12.50

CATALOGUE OF DOVER BOOKS

AN AUTOBIOGRAPHY, Margaret Sanger. Exciting personal account of hard-fought battle for woman's right to birth control, against prejudice, church, law. Foremost feminist document. 504pp. 5⅜ x 8½.
20470-7 Pa. $5.50

MY BONDAGE AND MY FREEDOM, Frederick Douglass. Born as a slave, Douglass became outspoken force in antislavery movement. The best of Douglass's autobiographies. Graphic description of slave life. Introduction by P. Foner. 464pp. 5⅜ x 8½. 22457-0 Pa. $5.50

LIVING MY LIFE, Emma Goldman. Candid, no holds barred account by foremost American anarchist: her own life, anarchist movement, famous contemporaries, ideas and their impact. Struggles and confrontations in America, plus deportation to U.S.S.R. Shocking inside account of persecution of anarchists under Lenin. 13 plates. Total of 944pp. 5⅜ x 8½.
22543-7, 22544-5 Pa., Two-vol. set $12.00

LETTERS AND NOTES ON THE MANNERS, CUSTOMS AND CONDITIONS OF THE NORTH AMERICAN INDIANS, George Catlin. Classic account of life among Plains Indians: ceremonies, hunt, warfare, etc. Dover edition reproduces for first time all original paintings. 312 plates. 572pp. of text. 6⅛ x 9¼. 22118-0, 22119-9 Pa.. Two-vol. set $12.00

THE MAYA AND THEIR NEIGHBORS, edited by Clarence L. Hay, others. Synoptic view of Maya civilization in broadest sense, together with Northern, Southern neighbors. Integrates much background, valuable detail not elsewhere. Prepared by greatest scholars: Kroeber, Morley, Thompson, Spinden, Vaillant, many others. Sometimes called Tozzer Memorial Volume. 60 illustrations, linguistic map. 634pp. 5⅜ x 8½.
23510-6 Pa. $10.00

HANDBOOK OF THE INDIANS OF CALIFORNIA, A. L. Kroeber. Foremost American anthropologist offers complete ethnographic study of each group. Monumental classic. 459 illustrations, maps. 995pp. 5⅜ x 8½.
23368-5 Pa. $13.00

SHAKTI AND SHAKTA, Arthur Avalon. First book to give clear, cohesive analysis of Shakta doctrine, Shakta ritual and Kundalini Shakti (yoga). Important work by one of world's foremost students of Shaktic and Tantric thought. 732pp. 5⅜ x 8½. (Available in U.S. only)
23645-5 Pa. $7.95

AN INTRODUCTION TO THE STUDY OF THE MAYA HIEROGLYPHS, Syvanus Griswold Morley. Classic study by one of the truly great figures in hieroglyph research. Still the best introduction for the student for reading Maya hieroglyphs. New introduction by J. Eric S. Thompson. 117 illustrations. 284pp. 5⅜ x 8½. 23108-9 Pa. $4.00

A STUDY OF MAYA ART, Herbert J. Spinden. Landmark classic interprets Maya symbolism, estimates styles, covers ceramics, architecture, murals, stone carvings as artforms. Still a basic book in area. New introduction by J. Eric Thompson. Over 750 illustrations. 341pp. 8⅜ x 11¼.
21235-1 Pa. $6.95

CATALOGUE OF DOVER BOOKS

GEOMETRY, RELATIVITY AND THE FOURTH DIMENSION, Rudolf Rucker. Exposition of fourth dimension, means of visualization, concepts of relativity as Flatland characters continue adventures. Popular, easily followed yet accurate, profound. 141 illustrations. 133pp. 5⅜ x 8½.
23400-2 Pa. $2.75

THE ORIGIN OF LIFE, A. I. Oparin. Modern classic in biochemistry, the first rigorous examination of possible evolution of life from nitrocarbon compounds. Non-technical, easily followed. Total of 295pp. 5⅜ x 8½.
60213-3 Pa. $4.00

PLANETS, STARS AND GALAXIES, A. E. Fanning. Comprehensive introductory survey: the sun, solar system, stars, galaxies, universe, cosmology; quasars, radio stars, etc. 24pp. of photographs. 189pp. 5⅜ x 8½. (Available in U.S. only)
21680-2 Pa. $3.75

THE THIRTEEN BOOKS OF EUCLID'S ELEMENTS, translated with introduction and commentary by Sir Thomas L. Heath. Definitive edition. Textual and linguistic notes, mathematical analysis, 2500 years of critical commentary. Do not confuse with abridged school editions. Total of 1414pp. 5⅜ x 8½.   60088-2, 60089-0, 60090-4 Pa., Three-vol. set $18.50

Prices subject to change without notice.

Available at your book dealer or write for free catalogue to Dept. GI, Dover Publications, Inc., 180 Varick St., N.Y., N.Y. 10014. Dover publishes more than 175 books each year on science, elementary and advanced mathematics, biology, music, art, literary history, social sciences and other areas.